Law Essentials

SCOTTISH COMMERCIAL LAW

EDINBURGH LAW ESSENTIALS

Series Editor: Nicholas Grier, Abertay University, Dundee

Scottish Commercial Law Essentials
Malcolm M Combe and Alisdair D J MacPherson

Scottish Legal System Essentials
Gerard Keegan

Delict Essentials
Francis McManus

Scottish Evidence Law Essentials
James Chalmers

Scottish Environmental Law Essentials
Francis McManus

Roman Law Essentials
Craig Anderson

Scottish Criminal Law Essentials
Claire McDiarmid

Legal Method Essentials for Scots Law
Dale McFadzean and Lynn Allardyce Irvine

Public Law Essentials
Jean McFadden and Dale McFadzean

Scottish Contract Law Essentials
Tikus Little

Scottish Family Law Essentials
Kenneth McK. Norrie

Private International Law Essentials
David Hill

Revenue Law Essentials
William Craig

Succession Law Essentials
Frankie McCarthy

Contract Law Essential Cases
Tikus Little

Trusts Law Essentials
John Finlay

Company Law Essentials
Josephine Bisacre and Claire McFadzean

Jurisprudence Essentials
Duncan Spiers

Human Rights Law Essentials
Valerie Finch and John McGroarty

Planning Law Essentials
Anne-Michelle Slater

Employment Law Essentials
Jenifer Ross

International Law Essentials
John Grant

Media Law Essentials
Douglas Maule and Zhongdong Niu

Intellectual Property Law Essentials
Duncan Spiers

European Law Essentials
Stephanie Switzer

Property Law Essentials
Duncan Spiers

Medical Law Essentials
Murray Earle

Scottish Administrative Law Essentials
Jean McFadden and Dale McFadzean

www.edinburghuniversitypress.com/series/ele

Law Essentials

SCOTTISH COMMERCIAL LAW

3rd edition

Malcolm M Combe and
Alisdair D J MacPherson

EDINBURGH
University Press

Edinburgh University Press is one of the leading university presses in the UK. We publish academic books and journals in our selected subject areas across the humanities and social sciences, combining cutting-edge scholarship with high editorial and production values to produce academic works of lasting importance. For more information visit our website: edinburghuniversitypress.com

First edition by David Cabrelli published in 2009 by Dundee University Press
Second edition by Malcolm M Combe published in 2013
by Dundee University Press
Reprinted in 2016 by Edinburgh University Press

Edinburgh University Press Ltd
The Tun – Holyrood Road
12(2f) Jackson's Entry
Edinburgh EH8 8PJ

Typeset in 10/13 Bembo by
IDSUK (DataConnection) Ltd

A CIP record for this book is available from the British Library

ISBN 978 1 3995 1177 3 (hardback)
ISBN 978 1 3995 1178 0 (paperback)
ISBN 978 1 3995 1179 7 (webready PDF)
ISBN 978 1 3995 1180 3 (epub)

CONTENTS

TABLE OF CASES

TABLE OF STATUTES

1   SALE OF GOODS

Prior to the enactment of the Sale of Goods Act 1893, the rules on the transfer of title of goods and implied warranties regarding the quality and fitness of goods were regulated by Scots common law. The common-law rules were particularly sophisticated and had been developed from civilian principles by the Scots judiciary since the Middle Ages. However, the majority of those rules were abandoned when the Sale of Goods Act 1893 was introduced in the late nineteenth century across the UK. Some of the current law in relation to sale of goods is now contained in a successor to that statute, the Sale of Goods Act 1979 ("SoGA").

SoGA regulated the contractual aspects of all sales of goods prior to 1 October 2015. SoGA was the source of relevant rules irrespective of the relative position of the transacting parties, meaning that SoGA applied whether the buyer was a consumer buying from a trader or a situation of two businesses transacting with each other. After 1 October 2015, SoGA continues to regulate non-consumer contracts for goods. The role of SoGA for matters relating to property law (ie title) has remained constant since its introduction.

The Consumer Rights Act 2015 ("CRA") was introduced to regulate aspects of contracts relating to goods – including contracts of sale – where a consumer transacts with a non-consumer (trader) with effect from 1 October 2015. A "consumer" is "an individual acting for purposes that are wholly or mainly outside that individual's trade, business, craft or profession". A similar but opposing definition applies to traders. This is set out in s 2 of CRA and discussed more fully below.

This means the Sale of Goods Act 1979 should be referred to for: (a) matters relating to property law; and (b) non-consumer contracts for the sale of goods. Non-consumer contracts of sale would involve: (i) two businesses transacting with each other; (ii) two non-businesses transacting with each other (a private sale); or (iii) a business buying from a non-business. The Consumer Rights Act 2015 is directed towards one party to a transaction (the consumer) obtaining goods from someone acting for purposes relating to that person's trade, business, craft or profession (the trader), rather than the type of transaction.

The approach taken in this chapter is to set out some themes which cut across consumer and non-consumer sales, before splitting the approach between non-consumer and consumer matters. The consumer content cross-refers to the relevant equivalent non-consumer rules when it is possible to do so. Until a dedicated body of case law is formed relating to the new consumer regime, recourse will need to be made to the position under SoGA for guidance.

THE CONTRACT OF SALE

Introduction

Pursuant to s 1(1) of SoGA, the statute relates only to contracts for the sale of goods as defined in s 2(1). This provides:

> "A contract of sale of goods is a contract by which the seller transfers or agrees to transfer the property in the goods to the buyer for a money consideration called the price."

Thus, there are five essential features of the contract of sale of goods, namely: (1) a contract of sale; (2) two parties – a buyer and a seller; (3) the conveyance of property (which may coincide with the contract of sale); (4) goods; and (5) the price.

Turning to consumers buying from traders, s 3 of CRA regulates relevant sales contracts (and also other consumer contracts relating to the supply of goods, such as hire). Section 5(1) of CRA tracks s 2(1) of SoGA, again requiring a transfer or agreement to transfer ownership and a price. Subject to minor differences, in relation to the definition of "goods" (discussed below) and a terminological difference of referring to a consumer and a trader, the same principles apply across both statutory regimes.

A contract of sale

It is fundamental that a contract must exist between a buyer and a seller. Hence, the usual rules of contract law will apply here, such as the requirements of offer and acceptance, an intention to create legal relations, and contractual capacity. Capacity to buy and sell is mentioned in s 3(1) of SoGA (CRA is silent on the matter), making it clear that this is covered by the general law of contract, but s 3(2) qualifies the standard position when "necessaries" (ie goods required for a person's day-to-day life – s 3(3)) are purchased by "a person who by reason of mental incapacity or drunkenness is incompetent to contract". In that situation, a "reasonable price" must be paid. There are no special formal requirements for a sale of goods contract (SoGA s 4(1)).

In terms of s 2(3) of SoGA, the contract may be conditional. Thus, the rights and obligations contained in it will require to be performed, and the contract purified, only on the satisfaction of a suspensive condition stipulated in the contract. Where a contract is subject to a suspensive condition or the contract stipulates that the seller will transfer title to the goods at some point in the future, s 2(5) of SoGA classifies such a contract as an "agreement to sell". Such an "agreement to sell" is nonetheless covered by SoGA. For consumer sales, "conditional sales contracts" are also regulated in terms of s 5(3) of CRA.

Neither contracts for the exchange of goods (ie goods for goods), which are referred to as "contracts of barter", nor gifts are covered by SoGA. Only a "sale", which is deemed to include "a bargain and sale" as well as "a sale and delivery" in terms of s 61(1), is covered by SoGA. Scots common law functions to regulate contracts of barter (that is to say, the exchange of goods) or donation (gifts). Moreover, other contracts which are similar to sale, but which fall outwith the compass of SoGA, are credit sale contracts, conditional sale contracts, contracts of hire or hire-purchase contracts. Some of these contracts are controlled by separate regulatory regimes such as the Supply of Goods and Services Act 1982. Meanwhile, as noted above, CRA operates to protect consumers who deal with traders, and such dealings would include hire and barter. Thus, the CRA rules discussed below about (for example) satisfactory quality in relation to a consumer sale would also apply to consumer hire.

A seller (or trader) and a buyer (or consumer)

Section 61(1) of SoGA defines a "seller" as someone who sells or agrees to sell and a "buyer" is a person who buys or agrees to buy goods. Similar definitions apply to consumer sales under s 5 of CRA, with the seller being classified as a trader and the buyer as a consumer within the CRA scheme. For ease "seller" and "buyer" will be used to represent traders acting as sellers and buyers acting as consumers respectively, except where the context requires otherwise.

Goods

As for the definition of "goods", s 61(1) of SoGA is the first aspect to consider. Here it is stipulated that "'goods' includes . . . all corporeal moveables except money; and in particular 'goods' includes emblements, industrial growing crops, and things attached to or forming part of the land which are agreed to be severed before sale or under the contract of sale and includes an undivided share in goods". Contracts for the supply of services do not fall within the compass of SoGA. In the case of *Robinson* v *Graves* (1935), the Court of Appeal ruled that a contract to paint a portrait was a contract for work and labour and not one for the sale of goods. "Corporeal moveables" are a categorisation of Scots property law, which can be simplified as physical objects that are not attached to the ground. The transfer of land is not regulated by SoGA. For industrial growing crops, see the case of *Boskabelle Ltd v Laird* (2006). It is possible a contract for the supply of computer software falls within SoGA (compare *Beta Computer Systems Europe Ltd v Adobe Computer Systems Europe Ltd* (1996) with *St Albans DC v International Computers Ltd* (1996) and *Erris Promotions Ltd v Commissioner of Inland Revenue* (2003); consider also *Software Incubator Ltd v Computer Associates (UK) Ltd* (2022), where (after a reference from the UK Supreme Court to the European Court of Justice) computer software was held to be goods in terms of a European directive relating to agency law).

There is a slightly different definition of "goods" in s 2(8) of CRA, namely: "any tangible moveable items, but that includes water, gas and electricity if and only if they are put up for supply in a limited volume or set quantity". "Tangible moveable" can be taken to mean "corporeal moveable". Notably, electricity is clearly included within "goods" for consumer sales. CRA contains specific provisions relating to digital goods. In relation to consumer purchases of computer software since 1 October 2015, these will be regulated by the rules about digital content in CRA, Part 1, Chapter 3.

Existing goods, future goods, specific goods and unascertained goods

Section 5 of SoGA makes a distinction between "existing goods" and "future goods", with CRA making similar provision in s 5(2).

Existing goods are defined in SoGA as goods which are "owned or possessed by the seller" at the time of formation of the contract of sale. Meanwhile, "future goods" are goods which are "to be manufactured or acquired by [the seller] after the making of the contract of sale". In the case of future goods, the contract of sale amounts to an agreement to sell. SoGA also distinguishes between "specific goods" and "unascertained goods", with the former being defined in s 61(1) of SoGA as "goods identified and agreed on at the time a contract of sale is made . . . includ[ing] an undivided share, specified as a fraction or percentage, of goods identified and agreed on as aforesaid", whereas unascertained goods are goods which are neither so identified or agreed. It is not possible to convey title in unascertained goods by virtue of s 16 of SoGA – only an agreement to sell unascertained goods can be formed. However, an exception applies in the case of s 20A of SoGA, where the contract is to sell unascertained goods which form part of an identified bulk, for example an earmarked crop of potatoes forming part of a larger bulk.

Price

A sale is predicated on there being a price. As such, parties must have agreed a price or price-fixing method, or a price may be determined by the course of dealing between the parties (SoGA, s 8(1)). Where no clear price can be determined, s 8(2) and (3) of SoGA state that the buyer must pay a reasonable price and a reasonable price is fact dependent. In the case of *Glynwed Distribution Ltd* v *S Koronka & Co Ltd* (1977), it was held that a reasonable price will be a price which is fair and just to the relevant parties to the contract – not necessarily the open market price.

TIME

In terms of s 10 of SoGA, subject to contrary agreement, stipulations as to time of payment are not of the essence in a contract of sale.

PASSING OF PROPERTY

Introduction

The object of a sale is to give the buyer a good (or unchallengeable) title to the goods sold. As will be discussed below, in every sale the seller is under an implied duty to supply goods which he has the right to sell (SGA s 12(1); CRA s 17(1)(b)). Prior to discussing that and indeed other implied terms, it is important to understand the law in relation to the transfer of ownership.

The Scots common law of sale of goods provided that the transfer of title from the seller to the buyer required the delivery of the goods and the will or intention of the seller to transfer. Delivery could be physical, constructive or symbolic. The common-law position can be contrasted with s 17(1) of SoGA which stipulates that where there is a contract for the sale of specific or ascertained goods the property in them is transferred to the buyer at such time as the parties to the contract intend it to be transferred. Thus, title to property passes with intention and intention is to be ascertained from the contract of sale. Where the intention of the parties cannot be ascertained, there are five rules contained in s 18 of SoGA which provide guidance. In the case of goods forming part of a bulk, subject to contrary agreement s 20A dictates when acquisition of a share of those goods occurs. Section 4 of CRA indicates that these property provisions also apply when a trader sells to a consumer.

The five rules

Rule 1 of s 18 of SoGA stipulates that where there is an unconditional contract for the sale of specific goods in a deliverable state the property in the goods passes to the buyer when the contract is made. Thus, provided the goods are specific in the sense described in s 61(1) of SoGA so that they are earmarked, title to the property will pass when an unconditional contract of sale is concluded despite the fact that delivery or payment of the price has not yet been made. Section 61(5) of SoGA states that the goods are deemed to be in a "deliverable state" where the buyer would, under the contract, be bound to take delivery of them. Subject to an exception which applies in the case of ss 20A and 20B of SoGA, s 61(1) provides that the word "delivery" denotes a "voluntary transfer of possession from one person to another".

Rule 2 directs that if something requires to be done to place specific goods into a state whereby the purchaser would be bound under the contract to take delivery, property will not pass in those goods until that thing is done. Here, one can envisage circumstances such as setting aside goods in sacks or bags or on pallets. Rule 3 takes the point a little further by stating that where goods require to be weighed, measured, tested, or some other act or thing needs to be done with reference to the goods for the purpose of ascertaining the price, the property does not pass until the act or thing is done and the buyer has notice that it has been done.

Rule 4 goes on to cover goods delivered to the purchaser on approval or on sale or return. Here, title to the goods is deemed to pass to the purchaser (i) when the purchaser signifies their approval or acceptance to the seller or does any other act adopting the transaction, or (ii) if the purchaser does not signify their approval or acceptance to the seller but retains the goods without giving notice of rejection, then, if a time has been fixed for the return of the goods, on the expiration of that time, or, if no time has been fixed, on the expiration of a reasonable notice.

Finally, rule 5 is drawn in terms of four segments and only the first will be dealt with here. It is to the effect that where there is a contract for the sale of unascertained or future goods by description, and goods of that description and in a deliverable state are unconditionally appropriated to the contract, either by the seller with the express or implied assent of the buyer or by the buyer with the assent of the seller, the property in the goods then passes to the buyer. In the case of *Carlos Federspiel & Co SA v Charles Twigg & Co Ltd* (1957), Pearson J remarked that in order to constitute an appropriation of the goods to the contract, the parties must have had, or be reasonably supposed to have had, an intention to attach the contract irrevocably to those goods, so that those goods and no others are the subject of the sale and become the property of the buyer.

Reservation of title

As a logical consequence of the rule that the property to the goods passes when the parties intend it to pass, s 19(1) of SoGA empowers the seller to reserve the right of disposal of the goods until certain conditions are fulfilled. Thus, a seller may stipulate that title is reserved in favour of the seller, notwithstanding delivery of the goods to the purchaser. The most obvious reason a seller might wish to retain title to the goods is to ensure that they receive payment from the purchaser. A contractual term called a "reservation of title clause" will achieve this. Here, property does not pass in the goods and remains with the seller until the purchaser pays the purchase price to the seller in full.

There are two kinds of retention of title clause, namely (1) the clause which provides that title will only pass to the purchaser once the price for those goods has been paid in full to the seller, and (2) the clause which provides that title will only pass to the purchaser once the price for those goods and all sums owing (in terms of other transactions) to the seller have been paid in full to the seller. The insertion of the first form of this clause simply renders a contract of sale subject to a suspensive condition and causes no difficulty for the Scottish courts: for example, see *Archivent Sales & Development Ltd v Strathclyde RC* (1985). However, the second form of clause, known as an "all sums" clause, was initially struck down by the Scottish courts as an attempt to create a security over corporeal moveables without possession in the case of *Deutz Engines Ltd v Terex Ltd* (1984). Yet in the case of *Armour v Thyssen Edelstahlwerke AG* (1990), the House of Lords (on appeal from the Court of Session) ruled that such "all sums" clauses were valid and simply another means of applying the rules in ss 17 and 19 of SoGA.

Third-party rights

The rights of third parties to property are also covered in SoGA. Section 21 of SoGA governs the situation where goods are sold by a non-owner. At the heart of the law lies a tension between the principle that someone's property rights should be protected (ie that an owner of goods should not be deprived of title where a third party purports to sell those goods to a buyer) and the principle that commercial transactions should be safeguarded (ie that a person who takes property from a non-owner of those goods in good faith and for value without notice should obtain a good title). The general rule in s 21(1) states that where goods are sold by a person who is not their owner, without the authority or the consent of the owner, the buyer acquires no better title to the goods than the seller had, unless the owner of the goods is by their conduct precluded from denying the seller's authority to sell. This is SoGA's way of articulating the classic principle *nemo dat quod non habet* which seeks to protect the property rights of the owner of the goods, that is that no one can pass a better title than that which they had.

However, there are exceptions to this general rule which seek to protect buyers of goods. The first exception is contained in the latter part of s 21(1) and applies where the real owner of the goods has taken action which personally bars them from challenging the non-owner's right to sell. The second exception is governed by s 24 of SoGA. In terms of this, if A sells goods to B but retains physical possession of the goods and then sells those same goods to C, C will take title to the goods provided that C is in good faith and has no notice of the prior sale to B. The third exception is contained in s 25(1) of SoGA and builds on s 24 by providing that a buyer in possession of goods which are still owned by a seller may give good title to those goods to a third-party purchaser, provided that that third-party purchaser is in good faith and has no notice of the rights of the seller in the goods (see *Archivent Sales & Development Ltd* v *Strathclyde RC* (1985)). So if A relinquishes possession of goods to B pursuant to a contract of sale and title remains with A, B nevertheless may confer good title on C where C buys the goods from B, provided C is in good faith and has no notice of the rights of A. Section 25(1) of SoGA can operate to defeat a seller's rights under a retention of title clause which they have included in a contract of sale, but the case of *National Employers Mutual General Insurance Association Ltd* v *Jones* (1990) makes clear that s 25 of SoGA does not have a blanket application to enable a seller A who did not have title to the goods to confer good title on C, for example where A had stolen the goods from Z.

Another exception to the general rule from a different statute may also be relevant. Section 2(1) of the Factors Act 1889 states that where a mercantile agent is in possession of goods or of the documents of title to goods with the consent of the owner, any sale of the goods made by them in the ordinary course of business will be sufficient to confer good title on a third-party purchaser, provided that that third party acts in good faith, and has no notice that the mercantile agent has no authority to sell the goods.

Separately, s 23 of SoGA sets out the rule where a seller has a voidable title to goods; that is to say, the seller is the owner, but that ownership right can be challenged by a particular party owing to the way in which that party lost ownership. This might be the case where the seller obtained their title in a transaction affected by slightly dubious circumstances but not so profoundly undermined as to make the whole arrangement void. If the seller's voidable title has not been avoided at the time of sale, the buyer obtains a good title provided he acts in good faith and without notice of the defect in title (*Macleod* v *Kerr* (1965)); where this is not the case, the buyer would also acquire a voidable title. Moreover, even if the title was somehow avoided, the buyer in possession of an object may be able to pass good title under the abovementioned s 25.

PASSING OF RISK

Introduction

Risk is a self-explanatory concept, relating to the party that bears any loss should goods come to harm or be destroyed. Under SoGA, but not under the CRA, the parties have the power to include a provision in their contract of sale which specifies when the risk of damage or destruction of goods passes from the seller to the purchaser. This need not be, but often is, coincidental with transfer of ownership. Where the parties fail to agree when risk is to pass, SoGA provides certain default rules which will apply. Section 20(1) of SoGA is to the effect that the goods remain at the seller's risk until title is transferred to the buyer and that once title is transferred to the buyer the goods are at the buyer's risk whether delivery has been made or not. Section 20(2) of SoGA goes on to state that where delivery has been delayed through the fault of either buyer or seller, the goods are at the risk of the party at fault as regards any loss which might not have occurred but for such fault. A good example of this principle is provided by the case of *Demby Hamilton & Co Ltd* v *Barden* (1949) where the buyer delayed in providing instructions as to the delivery of apple juice in casks. The apple juice went "off" and the delay of the buyer was used as a justification for the risk of deterioration to rest with the buyer although title in the goods remained with the seller.

Risk in a consumer sale

Where a trader is selling to a consumer, in terms of CRA s 29, the goods remain at the trader's risk until they come into the physical possession of either the consumer or a person identified by the consumer to take possession of the goods. The only circumstance where this rule does not apply is where the goods are delivered to a carrier who is commissioned by the consumer to deliver the goods and also that carrier is not a carrier the trader named as an option for the consumer. In terms of s 31(1) of CRA, it is not possible to contractually amend this statutory position.

THE SELLER'S DUTIES IN NON-CONSUMER SALES

Introduction

This section largely applies to commercial sale of goods or so-called "business to business" sales, but it also applies to sales between private individuals (except the rules under section 14). SoGA imposes a number of duties on the seller of goods in these circumstances. There are two principal duties.

Delivery

First, the seller must deliver the goods to the purchaser. The relevant rules are included in ss 27–30 of SoGA. Section 61 of SoGA defines "delivery" as "the voluntary transfer of possession from one person to another" rather than physical delivery of the goods.

Goods conform to contract of sale

The second principal duty of the seller is to provide goods which conform to the contract of sale. The contract of sale comprises express terms agreed by the parties and implied terms which are imposed into the parties' contract of sale by SoGA. These implied terms are specified in ss 12–15 of SoGA and confer a degree of protection in favour of purchasers.

Implied term as to title

Section 12(1) of SoGA stipulates that, subject to one particular exception, it is an implied term of a contract of sale that the seller has a right to sell the goods, and in the case of an agreement to sell that he will have such a right at the time when the property is to pass. Subsection (2) of s 12 goes on to provide that there is an implied term of the contract of sale that (i) the goods are free, and will remain free until the time when the property is to pass, from any charge or encumbrance not disclosed or known to the buyer before the contract is made, and (ii) the buyer will enjoy quiet possession of the goods except so far as it may be disturbed by the owner or other person entitled to the benefit of any charge or encumbrance so disclosed or known. Thus, if a seller purports to transfer title to goods where they do not have the right to sell them, the seller will be in breach of the contract of sale. However, where the seller's title to the goods or right to sell them is perfected subsequent to the sale, this will operate to cure the breach (for example, *Butterworth* v *Kingsway Motors Ltd* (1954)).

Consequences of breach of implied term as to title

Where the seller breaches the implied term to give good title to the goods in s 12(1) of SoGA, or indeed any other term of the contract, ss 15B(1) and 53A of SoGA provide that the non-consumer buyer's remedies are rejection of the goods and return of the price or damages.

Implied term as to sale by description

Section 13(1) of SoGA narrates that where there is a contract for the sale of goods by description, there is an implied term that the goods will correspond with the description. All online sales are deemed as a sale by description. A sale by description may be in images or numbers (for example, *Beale* v *Taylor* (1967)).

Although the word "description" covers words, images and numbers, it is insufficiently wide in scope to cover the capacity or power of the goods in the absence of an express specification (for example, *Border Harvesters Ltd* v *Edwards Engineering (Perth) Ltd* (1985)).

Implied term as to satisfactory quality

Section 14(2) of SoGA stipulates that where the goods are sold in the course of a business, there is an implied term that the goods supplied will be of satisfactory quality. The requirement that sales must be in the course of a business has been interpreted liberally (*MacDonald* v *Pollock* (2012)). Purely private sales fall outwith this definition: for example, an amateur musician selling a musical instrument to a friend. In terms of s 14(2A) of SoGA, goods are deemed to be of satisfactory quality if they meet the standard that a reasonable person would regard as satisfactory, taking account of any description of the goods, the price (if relevant) and all the other relevant circumstances. Section 14(2B) goes on to provide that the quality of goods includes their state and condition and the following (among others) are in appropriate cases aspects of the quality of goods:

(a) fitness for all the purposes for which goods of the kind in question are commonly supplied;

(b) appearance and finish;

(c) freedom from minor defects;

(d) safety; and

(e) durability.

The implied term in s 14(2C) of SoGA does not apply to any defect which is specifically drawn to the buyer's attention before the contract is made and, where the buyer examines the goods before the contract is made, the implied term does not cover any defect which that examination ought to reveal. As for how "satisfactory quality" is to be assessed, the cases of *Clegg* v *Andersson* (2003) and *Jewson Ltd* v *Boyhan* (2004) demonstrate that it is to be considered from the standpoint of the hypothetical reasonable person (which does not involve any assumption of expertise) and the assessment varies according to the nature of the goods and the persons to whom it is targeted.

The five factors Section 14(2B) of SoGA lists five pertinent factors. The first factor, namely "fitness for all the purposes for which goods of the kind in question are commonly supplied", overlaps with the separate statutory implied term of "fitness for a particular purpose" set out in s 14(3) of SoGA. The standard of "all common purposes" in s 14(2B)(a) of SoGA is a very high standard for the seller to discharge and so if goods are not fit for one of the purposes for which they are usually supplied, then the seller must make this fact known to the buyer. With regard to "appearance and finish" in s 14(2B)(b), shoddy workmanship in appearance and finish will be treated as a breach of the "satisfactory quality" implied term regardless of the sophistication, price and/or specification (or otherwise) of the goods. Section 14(2B)(c) of SoGA narrates that goods must be free from minor defects. For example, in the case of *Lamarra* v *Capital Bank plc* (2006), a Range Rover had a number of minor defects, namely: when driven, the vehicle pulled to the left, causing undue tyre wear; the layout of the pedals was faulty; there was a loud noise from the engine or transmission system; there was a deep scratch on the ashtray; the glove box was incorrectly fitted; the paintwork on parts of the roof was poorly finished; and the navigation disc was missing. It was held that the Range Rover was not free from minor defects and so the statutory implied term of satisfactory quality had been breached. Moreover, the court stated that the reasonableness or otherwise of the buyer's conduct cannot be relevant to the determination of satisfactory quality. However, the court did say that the implied term of satisfactory quality and the factor of freedom from minor defects do not entitle a purchaser in law to expect perfection in the goods supplied. *Lamarra* can be contrasted quite sharply with the decisions in the earlier cases of *Millars of Falkirk* v *Turpie* (1976) and *Bernstein* v *Pamson Motors (Golders Green) Ltd* (1987) where the attitude of the judiciary was to the effect that the law expected buyers of motor vehicles simply to put up with minor defects. It is likely that the courts would follow *Lamarra* in modern times.

The final component of the seller's duty to provide goods of a satisfactory quality is contained in s 14(2B)(d) and (e) of SoGA. Here, it is stipulated that goods must be safe and durable. In relation to the criterion of durability, the case of *Thain* v *Anniesland Trade Centre* (1997) is a cause for concern for purchasers of second-hand vehicles. There, it was ruled that durability was not a quality reasonably to be expected of a second-hand car where a faulty gear box rendered the car a write-off two weeks subsequent to its purchase.

Implied term of fitness for purpose

Section 14(3) of SoGA complements s 14(2) by providing that goods supplied must be reasonably fit for the particular purpose to which they are to be put where this is made known to the seller by the purchaser (expressly or by implication), whether or not that is a purpose for which such goods are commonly supplied, except where the circumstances show that the buyer does not rely, or that it is unreasonable for them to rely, on the skill or judgement of the seller or credit-broker. In *Jewson Ltd* v *Boyhan* (2004), the court clarified the respective roles of s 14(3) and (2B)(a) of SoGA. The former is relevant to impose a particular obligation tailored to the particular circumstances of a particular case, whereas the latter serves to impose an obligation on a seller for breach of the duty to provide goods of satisfactory quality where the purpose for which the goods are to be used is a common purpose. A final point to make is that goods will not be deemed to be unfit for purpose where, due to an idiosyncrasy in the buyer or the buyer's property, there would appear to be a defect in the goods. For example, in the case of *Griffiths* v *Peter Conway Ltd* (1939), it was held that a Harris tweed coat was not defective where the purchaser contracted dermatitis by wearing it and it could be proven that the purchaser had abnormally sensitive skin. If the coat had been worn by a person with normal skin, it was clear that no dermatitis would have been contracted by that person.

Implied term as to sales by sample

The final implied term of the contract of sale is set out in s 15 of SoGA. Section 15(2)(a) and (c) of SoGA provide that, in the case of a contract for sale by sample, there is an implied term that (i) the bulk must correspond to the sample in quality and (ii) the goods must be free from any defect which renders their quality unsatisfactory, which would not be apparent on a reasonable examination of the sample. Section 15(1) stipulates that a contract of sale is a contract for sale by sample where there is an express or implied term to that effect in the contract.

THE NON-CONSUMER BUYER'S REMEDIES

Where the seller has breached one of the statutory duties in SoGA or one of the express terms of the contract of sale, there are a number of options available to the buyer, namely: right to damages (s 15B(1)(a)); right to rescind and reject all of the goods if the breach is material (s 15B(1)(b), and note in *Clegg* v *Andersson* (2003), it was ruled that a buyer has a free choice to seek damages or rejection); right to accept some of the goods and reject some of the goods if some of the goods are not in conformity with the contract of sale (s 35A(1)); and right to an order of specific implement where the seller has breached their obligation to deliver specific or ascertained goods (s 52(1)). SoGA also makes specific provision for what happens in the event of the wrong quantity of goods being delivered (s 30).

Measure of damages

Sections 51(2) and 53A(1) of SoGA stipulate that the measure of the non-consumer buyer's damages on a breach of an express or implied term of the contract of sale (in terms of s 15B(1)) is the estimated loss directly and naturally arising, in the ordinary course of events, from the seller's breach – whether the goods were delivered or not. Where an action is raised for damages on non-delivery of the goods and there is an available market for the goods, s 51(3) of SoGA states that the measure of damages is *prima facie* to be ascertained by the difference between the contract price and the market or current price of the goods at the time or times when they ought to have been delivered or, if no time was fixed, at the time of the refusal to deliver. Where the goods are delivered and are defective, how this is calculated depends on whether the buyer rejects or retains the defective goods. If the buyer rejects the defective goods, damages will be calculated on the basis that the goods have not been delivered, that is in terms of s 51(3) set out above. However, s 53A(2) of SoGA provides that if the buyer retains the defective goods, the damages will be the difference between the value of the goods at the time of delivery and their value had the contract been fulfilled.

The buyer's right of rejection

A buyer will have lost the right to reject when they have accepted the goods or are deemed to have accepted the goods. Section 35(1) of SoGA provides that the buyer is deemed to have accepted the goods when intimation is given to the seller to that effect or when they take delivery of the goods and do any act in relation to them which is inconsistent with ownership remaining with the seller (see *Fiat Auto Financial Services* v *Connelly* (2007)). In terms of s 35(2) of SoGA, the buyer is not deemed to have accepted the goods where they have not previously examined them until they have had a reasonable opportunity of examining them for the purpose of ascertaining whether they conform to the contract of sale and, in the case of contract for sale by sample, of comparing the bulk with the sample. In the case of *Henry Pini & Co* v *George Smith & Co* (1895), it was ruled that it is likely that once the reasonable opportunity to examine has passed, the right to reject will be lost. The buyer is also deemed to have accepted the goods when, after the lapse of a reasonable time, they retain the goods without intimating to the seller that they have rejected them.

For further guidance on what constitutes a reasonable period of time, one must look to the case law. However, the difficulty with it is that it paints no clear picture as to what period of time is "reasonable" and much depends on the nature of the goods acquired (see *Bernstein* v *Pamson Motors (Golders Green) Ltd* (1987)), the balancing of the opposing interests of the buyer and seller (see *Truk (UK) Ltd* v *Tokmakidis GmbH* (2000), per Raymond Jack J), the whole circumstances of the case and other factors. For example, in the case of *Bernstein* v *Pamson Motors (Golders Green) Ltd* (1987) a period of 3 weeks in the case of the purchase of a new Nissan Laurel motor car (140 miles having been clocked up) was held not to be a reasonable period of time and accordingly it was held that the right of rejection had been lost. *Bernstein* can be contrasted with *Rogers* v *Parish (Scarborough) Ltd* (1987), where it was held that a purchaser had not lost his right to reject when a Range Rover motor vehicle was rejected 6 months subsequent to the date of purchase and had clocked up in excess of 5,500 miles in that period. A similar approach was adopted in *Truk (UK) Ltd* v *Tokmakidis GmbH* (2000) where the purchasers of a chassis and underlift were entitled to reject 7 months after the date of conclusion of the contract, whereas in *Douglas* v *Glenvarigill Co Ltd* (2010) 15 months was not a reasonable time to reject a car suffering from a latent defect. More recently, *Combe* v *Pert's House Furnishers Ltd* (2018) (which related to furniture that was not of satisfactory quality) suggests a lack of interaction between the parties for 6 or 7 months would be enough to allow a seller to reach "commercial closure" such that rejection will not be available.

Section 35(6) of SoGA provides further guidance with regard to the expiry of the buyer's right to reject. Here, it is stated that a buyer does not lose their right to reject merely because the seller and buyer have agreed to the repair of the goods. Where the goods are repaired, but the seller refuses to disclose the nature of the defect to the buyer, *J & H Ritchie Ltd* v *Lloyd Ltd* (2007) decided that the buyer did not lose his right to reject the repaired machinery subsequently even though the seller refused to disclose the nature of the defect and limited disclosure to informing the buyer that the goods had been repaired to "factory gate specification".

THE BUYER'S DUTIES

The duties of the buyer are threefold in terms of the Act. First, to accept the goods. Second, to pay the price in accordance with the contract of sale in terms of s 27 of the Act. In terms of s 10 of the Act, time is not usually of the essence in contracts of sale. The effect of this rule is that the seller will not have the right to rescind if payment is not made timeously. Finally, the buyer is under a duty to take delivery of the goods within a reasonable period of time in terms of s 37 of the Act.

THE SELLER'S REMEDIES

Notwithstanding the fact that ownership of the goods has passed to the buyer, s 39(1) of the Act provides that the seller is entitled to exercise the following possessory remedies when they have not been paid:

- a lien on the goods or a right to retain them for the price while they are in possession of them;
- in the case of the insolvency of the buyer, a right of stopping the goods in transit after they have parted with the possession of them; and/or
- a right of re-sale.

Separately, the seller can sue for the price where either "the property in the goods has passed to the buyer and he wrongfully neglects or refuses to pay for the goods" (s 49(1) of SoGA) or "the price is payable on a day certain irrespective of delivery and the buyer wrongfully neglects or refuses to pay such price" (s 49(2)). Under s 50 of SoGA, the seller can claim damages for non-acceptance equal to "the estimated loss directly and naturally resulting" from the buyer's breach of contract.

CONSUMER SALE

Introduction

The Consumer Rights Act 2015 provides a full statutory framework for consumer rights, including in sale of goods situations. As noted above, this regime applies when a consumer (someone not acting in accordance with a trade, business or profession) buys goods from a trader (acting in accordance with a trade, business or profession). CRA also includes a specific regime for digital content, defined in s 2 as data which are produced and supplied in digital form, which will be discussed below.

Statutory rights

The consumer has a number of statutory rights which cannot be contracted out of (in terms of s 31 CRA). Some of these are analogous to provisions in SoGA and relevant case law can be referred to for guidance. These analogous provisions are that goods: are of satisfactory quality (CRA s 9, analogous to SoGA s 14(2), subject to an additional point noted below); are fit for a particular purpose (CRA s 10, see SoGA s 14(3)); are as described (CRA s 11, see SoGA s 13); and match any sample (CRA s 13, see SoGA s 15). Further, the trader must have the right to transfer the goods under s 17 CRA, as discussed above in relation to the property law implications of a sale.

In a consumer context, the implied term of satisfactory quality is augmented slightly as compared to the non-consumer situation. In both regimes, the quality of goods is satisfactory if they meet the standard that a reasonable person would consider satisfactory, taking account of (a) any description of the goods, (b) the price for the goods, and (c) all the other relevant circumstances. What differs is that s 9(5) CRA details that relevant circumstances include any public statement about the specific characteristics of the goods made by the trader, the producer or any representative of the trader or the producer, including in advertising or labelling (s 9(6)), subject to exceptions where such statements were not actually relevant or known to the trader (s 9(7)).

There are some further implied terms that have no direct analogy to SoGA. Goods that are ultimately supplied must match any model seen or examined by the consumer (CRA s 14). This is slightly different to a sample, in that it is not the specific item which was on trial or demonstrated that the consumer acquires. Under s 12 CRA, there is also an implied term that goods conform to certain pre-contract information. This is to the effect that where information must be provided under the Consumer Contracts (Information, Cancellation and Additional Charges) Regulations 2013 (SI 2013/3134) by the trader to the consumer before the contract, such information is to be treated as included as a term of the contract. The nature of the information depends on the nature of the transaction (for example, in a shop or by electronic means) and (in relation to s 12) refers to pre-contract information such as price, delivery and complaints handling. (Separately, those regulations can apply to afford consumers rights of cancellation for transactions that take place away from a trader's premises, as noted below.) A consumer also has a right such that the goods must be appropriately installed if required by the contract (CRA s 15). Finally, where goods are sold with digital content then the goods will not conform to the contract if the digital content is itself not in conformance with the contract (CRA s 16). Section 18 of CRA provides there are no further implied terms about the quality of the goods or their fitness for any particular purpose, but other contractual terms can be expressly agreed (provided they do not undermine consumer protection) or there may be other implied terms from other statutes.

Consumer remedies

A consumer will have certain remedies when goods do not conform to the contract, as detailed in s 19 of CRA. Lack of conformity is measured at the date of delivery and within 6 months in certain circumstances (under s 19(14) and (15)). Consumers may have different options, with two rights of rejection introduced by section 20 CRA, depending on how long ago they received the goods in question. Potential options include: (a) the short-term right to reject (ss 20 and 22); (b) the right to repair or replacement (s 23); and (c) the right to a price reduction or the final right to reject (ss 20 and 24).

The short-term right to reject

The powerful short-term right to reject is generally only available for 30 days (s 22(3) of CRA), and does not apply in a situation where the contractual breach is under s 15 (where installation of the goods was part of the contract and installation has not been performed correctly). All a consumer need do is intimate rejection clearly (s 20(5)–(6)) and a refund of the price must be forthcoming without undue delay and in any event within 14 days beginning with the day on which the trader agrees that the consumer is entitled to a refund (s 20(15)). In addition to imposing a duty on the trader to provide a refund, s 20(7) stipulates that the consumer has a duty to make the goods available for collection by the trader or (if there is an agreement for the consumer to return rejected goods) to return them as agreed. Where the consumer has clearly intimated a properly made rejection and attempted to follow this up with suitable correspondence, this duty does not operate on an open-ended basis and in due course such a consumer will be entitled to do as they wish with the goods (*Johnston v R & J Leather (Scotland) Ltd* (2019)). The trader must bear any reasonable costs of returning them, other than any costs relating to returning the goods in person to the place where physical possession was initially transferred. Partial rejection is covered in s 21.

Right to repair or replacement

The buyer may opt for either a repair or replacement, or the decision may be forced on the buyer because 30 days have expired and as such the comparatively clean short-term right to reject is no longer available. Repair (that is, correcting the issue with the goods such that they do conform with the contract) or replacement is regulated by s 23 CRA. Importantly, in terms of s 23(3) the trader cannot be forced to repair or replace where one of those is impossible or the consumer's choice is disproportionate (considering the terms of s 23(4), including unreasonable costs for the trader, when compared to the alternative of those remedies). If the consumer requires the trader to repair or replace the goods, s 23(2) provides the trader must do so within a reasonable time and without significant inconvenience to the consumer, with reasonable time and significant inconvenience depending on the nature of the goods and the purpose for which the goods were acquired. The trader is to bear any necessary costs incurred in relation to this (including any labour, materials or postage). A consumer who requires or agrees to a repair or replacement can only revisit this choice if a reasonable time to repair or replace has been afforded.

Right to price reduction or final right to reject

The backstop of section 24 can apply where the first two remedies cannot be (or have not been) carried out. Section 24(5) provides that a consumer who has the right to a price reduction and the final right to reject may only exercise one (not both), and is only entitled to do so where:

(a) after one repair or one replacement, the goods do not conform to the contract;

(b) because of section 23(3) the consumer can require neither repair nor replacement of the goods; or

(c) the consumer has required the trader to repair or replace the goods, but the trader is in breach of the requirement of section 23(2)(a) to do so within a reasonable time and without significant inconvenience to the consumer.

How much of a price reduction is appropriate appears to be something that is open to interpretation, but it does seem from the drafting that a 100 per cent reduction could be appropriate (s 24(2) CRA). Price reduction will not be appropriate at all where goods cannot be given back in their original state or cannot be divided up to provide the appropriate reduction (s 24(4) CRA).

In the event of the consumer exercising the final right to reject, the process is similar to the short-term right to reject (albeit the consumer can wait for up to 6 months and still have a chance of a full refund, rather than having 30 days to act). Any refund to the consumer after rejection may be reduced by a "deduction for use" (s 24(8)), to take account of the use the consumer has had of the goods in the period since they were delivered, but that deduction is in turn regulated by subsections (9) (no deduction if the only reason the consumer had the goods was a failure to collect) and (10) (no deduction in the first 6 months, unless the goods are a motor vehicle or another specified item). How the deduction is to be calculated is not stated, but it may be that principles drawn from earlier legislation (such as the now repealed ss 48A–48F of the Sale of Goods Act 1979) could be relevant.

Other rules about remedies

There are provisions in the statute about delivery of the wrong quantity and the consumer's option to reject or retain what is delivered at the contract rate (s 25(1) (too little) and s 25(2) (too much)). Note also that nothing in CRA prevents a consumer, for example, seeking specific implement (see s 19(9)–(11)).

Trader remedies

No statutory remedies are provided for a trader in CRA. A trader has to look to the standard contractual remedies.

Digital content

The purchase of digital content is subject to a similar but different regime as physical goods under CRA, as detailed in Part 1 of Chapter 3 of the statute. Implied terms exist in relation to familiar aspects such as satisfactory quality (s 34) and fitness for a particular purpose (s 35), and there are also context specific rules, for example in relation to transmission and facilities for continued transmission (s 39). Specific remedies of repair or replacement, the right to a price reduction and a right to refund are provided for in s 42, and it is clarified that these do not exclude the consumer from pursuing a remedy through another route (such as a claim for damages). There is also a remedy provided for the situation where a trader supplies digital content to a consumer and the digital content causes damage to a device or to other digital content (s 46).

Unfair contract terms and consumers

CRA also makes provision about unfair contractual terms in a trader and consumer situation more generally (replacing the regime that preceded it in the Unfair Contract Terms Act 1977). The need for such rules in a consumer sale of goods situation is mitigated by s 31 CRA, which prevents the amendment of CRA's implied terms, the rules around allocation and rules relating to delivery for a goods contract where that would be to the consumer's detriment. It is not beyond the realms of possibility that other unfair terms could nevertheless be dreamed up by a trader, and if such would not be binding on a consumer (in accordance with s 62 CRA). According to s 62(4) CRA, a term is unfair if, contrary to the requirement of good faith, it causes a significant imbalance in the parties' rights and obligations under the contract to the detriment of the consumer, and s 63 (together with Schedule 2) details provisions that may or must be regarded as unfair.

Other consumer provisions

In addition to rights and associated remedies in CRA, a consumer purchase benefits from other statutory rights. The Consumer Protection from Unfair Trading Regulations 2008 (SI 2008/1277) prohibits unfair commercial practices by traders against consumers, and can offer redress to consumers when there has been a misleading action (through the provision of false or deceptive information) or an aggressive practice (such that a consumer's freedom of choice is impaired). There are also rules against charging a consumer for certain payment methods in the Consumer Rights (Payment Surcharges) Regulations 2012 (SI 2012/3110) and regulating excessive charges over and above the main subject-matter of the sale in the Consumer Contracts (Information, Cancellation and Additional Charges) Regulations 2013. These latter regulations, which were mentioned above in the context of the information supplied to a consumer and the need for that to be accurate to comply with s 12 CRA, can also provide a right to cancel contracts concluded at a distance or away from a trader's trading outlet.

Essential Facts

- A contract of sale of goods is a contract by which the seller transfers or agrees to transfer the property in the goods to the buyer for a money consideration called the price.
- The word "goods" includes all corporeal moveables except money, emblements, industrial growing crops, and things attached to or forming part of the land which are agreed to be severed before sale or under the contract of sale and includes an undivided share in goods.
- Where there is a contract for the sale of specific or ascertained goods the property in them is transferred to the buyer at such time as the parties to the contract intend it to be transferred.

- Where the intention of the parties cannot be ascertained, there are five rules contained in s 18 of the Act which determine whether title to the goods has passed.
- Sales by a trader (acting in the course of a trade, business of profession) to a consumer (not acting in such a course) are subject to a dedicated statutory regime.
- In a non-consumer sale, the goods remain at the seller's risk until title is transferred to the buyer and once title is transferred to the buyer the goods are at the buyer's risk whether delivery has been made or not. In a consumer sale, the goods remain at the seller's risk until they come into the physical possession of either the consumer or a person identified by the consumer to take possession of the goods.
- The seller must provide goods which conform to the contract of sale.
- The seller must comply with the statutory implied terms, with different terms applying where the buyer is a consumer buying from a trader.
- Where the seller breaches an express term or one of the statutory implied terms, a non-consumer buyer will have a right to damages, a right to rescind and reject all of the goods if the breach is material, the right to accept some of the goods and reject some of the goods (if appropriate) or the right to obtain a decree of specific implement.
- A consumer buyer has a short-term right to reject goods that can be exercised within 30 days, a right to have the goods repaired or replaced, a right to a price reduction or a final right to reject.
- A buyer will have lost the right to reject when he has accepted the goods or is deemed to have accepted the goods.

Essential Cases

Robinson v Graves (1935): a contract to paint a portrait was a contract for work and labour and not one for the sale of goods.

Beale v Taylor (1967): a car advertised by model and year was sufficient to constitute a sale by description.

Clegg v Andersson (2003) and **Jewson Ltd v Boyhan (2004)**: "satisfactory quality" is to be considered from the standpoint of the hypothetical reasonable person and the assessment varies according to the nature of the goods and the persons to whom it is targeted.

Lamarra v Capital Bank plc (2006): where a Range Rover had minor defects, it was held that the statutory implied term of satisfactory quality had been breached.

Thain v Anniesland Trade Centre (1997): durability was not a quality reasonably to be expected of a second-hand car where a faulty gear box rendered the car a write-off 2 weeks subsequent to its purchase.

Fiat Auto Financial Services v Connelly (2007): a buyer's continued use of a vehicle as a taxi for several months did not amount to acts inconsistent with ownership of the seller where the buyer was liaising with the seller regularly with regard to concerns over the vehicle's fitness for purpose.

Henry Pini & Co v George Smith & Co (1895): it is likely that once the reasonable opportunity to examine the goods has passed, the right of the buyer to reject the goods will be lost.

Bernstein v Pamson Motors (Golders Green) Ltd (1987): where the purchaser of a new Nissan Laurel motor car (140 miles having been clocked up) attempted to reject the goods after a period of 3 weeks, this was held not to be a reasonable period of time within which to reject.

Rogers v Parish (Scarborough) Ltd (1987): it was ruled that a purchaser had not lost his right to reject when he rejected a Range Rover motor vehicle (which had clocked up in excess of 5,500 miles) 6 months subsequent to the date of purchase.

Truk (UK) Ltd v Tokmakidis GmbH (2000): held that the purchasers of a chassis and underlift were entitled to reject 7 months after the date of conclusion of the contract.

J & H Ritchie Ltd v Lloyd Ltd (2007): a buyer did not lose his right to reject repaired machinery where the seller refused to disclose the nature of the defect and limited disclosure to informing the buyer that the goods had been repaired to "factory gate specification".

MacDonald v Pollock (2012): a liberal interpretation is appropriate when ascertaining what is meant by a seller in the course of business.

2 HIRE

A contract of hire is a special type of contract, which is one form of a contract of "location" (Stair, *Institutions*, I, 15, 1). Certain implied terms in law are incorporated into contracts of hire by the common law and ss 11G–11L of the Supply of Goods and Services Act 1982 (the "1982 Act"), much in the same way as certain implied terms in law are implied into every contract for the sale of goods by virtue of the Sale of Goods Act 1979. That being said, and in the same way that implied terms in the Sale of Goods Act 1979 do not apply to sales from a trader to consumer, a consumer who hires an item from a trader benefits from the same implied terms and remedies as a consumer buyer does under the Consumer Rights Act 2015 (subject to necessary changes to reflect the nature of hire as compared to sale). Consumer hire is brought into the Consumer Rights Act 2015 by the operation of s 3 (with s 6) of that statute. The focus of this chapter is accordingly on non-consumer hire, save where it is necessary to raise consumer matters not already considered in the previous chapter. Consumer credit considerations can also be relevant in a consumer hire situation, which will be touched on in this chapter but reference should also be made to Chapter 8 below.

Section 11G of the 1982 Act defines a contract for the hire of goods as a contract under which one person hires or agrees to hire goods to another, other than a hire-purchase agreement. "Lessor" means the supplier, while "lessee" means the person hiring the goods (sometimes referred to as the "hirer").

TYPES OF HIRE CONTRACT

Finance lease

There are a number of modern forms of the contract of hire. One is the finance lease, where a lessee selects goods from a supplier and the lessor purchases those goods from the supplier and hires them to the lessee for a specific period in return for rental payments. Thus, the lessor acts as purchaser vis-à-vis the supplier and lessor vis-à-vis the lessee. To that extent, the lessor acts as financier and the rental payments cover the lessor's aggregate capital costs of providing the goods to the lessee, the lessor's expenses and a margin in respect of the lessor's profit for acting as financier.

Operating lease

In the case of an operating lease, the lessee seeks to use an asset for a proportion of its economic life and there is no intention that they will acquire ownership of the asset. The payments made by the lessee therefore take account of the property being returned to the lessor at the end of the agreement. The lessor assumes some of the risk that the value of the equipment let to the lessee will be inadequate at the end of the lease and they may be able to subsequently lease it again to the same lessee or to another party or alternatively sell the property to recoup their investment.

Contract hire

Another type of contract of hire is contract hire. Contract hire is usually encountered in the context of the hire of commercial vehicles. In terms of this contract, a finance house will let a vehicle to an employer for 3 years for use by the employees. The rent is pitched at a level which is sufficient to cover the acquisition cost of the car or vehicle minus the estimated residual value of the car or vehicle to the finance house at the termination of the 3-year period.

Rental or hire agreement

The rental or hire agreement is often used in respect of goods or equipment used by businesses. The rental or hire agreement may endure for a short- or long-term period, depending on the nature of the equipment. The owner/lessor will commonly provide various warranties as to the condition and fitness for purpose of the goods and also provide maintenance and servicing assistance. To that extent, the owner/lessor will maintain some responsibility towards the hirer in respect of the proper functioning of those goods.

THE ESSENTIALS OF THE CONTRACT OF HIRE

Stair stipulates that there are three essential elements to the contract of hire, namely a thing to be let, a rent agreed upon and finally the consent of the contracting parties (Stair, *Institutions*, I, 15, 1). To these three requirements, Bell adds a fourth factor, namely a specified period of let (Bell, *Commentaries*, I, 481). Any moveables may qualify as the thing let, so long as the nature of the goods is such that they are not consumable. The rent should be in money, rather than money's worth. However, in the case of *Wilson* v *Orr* (1879), the Court of Session was content to classify the hire of a horse in return for a rent consisting of providing the horse's keep as a contract of hire. The final requisite factor, namely the consent of the contracting parties, may manifest itself verbally or in writing. However, where the contract of hire qualifies as a consumer hire agreement in terms of s 15 of the

Consumer Credit Act 1974 (the "1974 Act"), ss 60 and 61 of the 1974 Act direct that the agreement must be reduced to writing.

COMMON-LAW IMPLIED TERMS

Introduction

In a contract of hire, unless specifically varied otherwise, there are implied terms which impose reciprocal obligations on both lesser and lessee.

Lessor's common-law obligations

First, we will consider the common-law implied terms which impose obligations on the lessor.

Duty to deliver

The first implied term to mention is the lessor's duty to deliver the subjects of hire in a state of good condition and repair (*Wilson* v *Norris* (1810)). The expenses of delivery must be borne by the lessor. The doctrine of *rei interitus* applies to the contract for the hire of goods in much the same way as the contract for the lease of heritable property. That is to say that where the subjects of hire are destroyed and delivery is no longer possible, the lessee will no longer wield the right to force the lessor to render such delivery.

Duty not to interfere

Second, the lessor must not interfere with the lessee's enjoyment of the subjects of hire and warrants against such interference. The rationale behind this rule is that the lessor must not impede the lessee's enjoyment of the thing hired. To that extent, the lessor warrants their title to the goods. However, where possession is lost by the lessee as a result of the lessor breaching their warranty against such interference, the effect is that the contract of hire is terminated, no further rent is payable by the lessee and the lessee is entitled to claim damages from the lessor.

Duty to keep goods in good order and repair

Third, the lessor has a duty to keep the goods hired in sufficiently good order and repair. The purpose of this implied term is to ensure that the lessee has the ability to continue to use the goods hired throughout the period of hire. Some minor repairs must be borne, however, by the lessee: for example, in the case of the hire of a vehicle, the lessee will be under an obligation to change the tyres and meet the cost of doing so. During the period that the goods are undergoing repair and the lessee does not have use of the goods, the lessee will be entitled to an abatement of rent. However, there are exceptions to this rule: for example, where a car breaks down where it is subject to a long-term hire contract, the rent will probably not be subject to an abatement (*Wilson* v *Norris* (1810)).

Warranty as to freedom from defects

Finally, the common law provides that the lessor is under an obligation to warrant that the goods let are free from defects: that is, that the goods are fit for ordinary uses and purposes or for any particular uses in the contemplation of the parties. However, it is subject to doubt whether the lessor is under continuing liability for latent defects. Bell's *Principles*, s 141 states that there is no continuing liability for latent defects where the lessor was unaware of them or could not reasonably have known of them. However, in *Wilson* v *Norris* (1810), the opposite view was taken.

Exception for finance leases and operating leases

Where the contract of hire qualifies as a finance lease or an operating lease, the contract will be treated as a *sui generis* contract (ie not as a contract of hire) and so the above implied term that the lessor has a good unencumbered title to the goods will not be implied into those contracts (*G M Shepherd Ltd* v *North West Securities Ltd* (1991)). That is, where a finance lessor is not involved in the selection of the hired goods, the contract will not amount to the nominate contract of hire and so the implied term that the lessor has a duty to warrant that the goods let are free from defects will not apply. However, whether the result of *G M Shepherd* is that all of the implied terms of the contract of hire do not apply to the finance lease or operating lease is not particularly clear.

Lessee's common-law obligations

There are essentially five common-law obligations imposed on a lessee.

Duty to take delivery

The lessee is under an obligation to take delivery of the goods hired. Where the lessee breaches this obligation, the lessor is entitled to seek damages and terminate the contract. The alternative remedy is specific implement.

Duty to pay rent

Second, the lessee must pay the rent. Usually, the rent will be paid in arrears. However, the contract or custom may provide or indicate otherwise.

Subject to exceptions, where the lessee is temporarily deprived of the use and enjoyment of the thing hired, he will have the right to a rent abatement.

Duty to use the goods for the purpose for which they were let

Third, there is an implied term to the effect that the lessee must use the goods hired for the purpose for which they were let. In the case of *Seton* v *Paterson* (1880) where a horse was hired for the purpose of undertaking a day's journey, but it was taken for a gallop race by the lessee, the lessee was held to be in breach of this implied term. The same point would apply to cars in modern times.

Duty to take proper care of the goods

Fourth, the lessee is under a duty to take proper care of the goods hired (Stair, *Institutions*, I, 15, 5). The lessee is not liable for casual or accidental perishing of the goods hired. In *Campbell* v *Lord Kennedy* (1828) the lessee of a horse was deemed to be in breach of the implied term where he lent it to a friend whose actions resulted in the horse catching a chill and dying. However, if the goods deteriorate due to fair wear and tear or the goods are damaged as a result of something which was not the lessee's fault, the lessee will not have breached this implied term. If the goods perish in circumstances which were not the fault of the lessee, the lessor must take the risk of such destruction (*Jacksons (Edinburgh) Ltd* v *Constructors John Brown Ltd* (1965)).

Duty to restore the thing hired in a good state of condition and repair

Finally, the lessee has a duty to restore the thing hired to the lessor in a good state of condition and repair. This implied term complements the implied term that the lessee is under a duty to take proper care of the goods hired during the period of hire. As explained by Lord Justice-Clerk Moncrieff in *Wilson* v *Orr* (1879), if the lessee is able to discharge the latter implied term, they will stand in good stead for the purposes of the implied term of restoring the thing let in good condition towards the end of the period of hire. Of course, where damage is caused to the goods which was not the lessee's fault, the lessee is not liable to the lessor, provided the lessee is able to justify and explain the loss. Where the lessee cannot explain or justify the loss, they will be liable to the lessor for the value of the goods lost.

STATUTORY REGULATION OF THE CONTRACT OF HIRE

Consumer hire agreements

Where a contract of hire qualifies as a consumer hire agreement in terms of s 15(1) of the 1974 Act, consumer credit implications will arise. The agreement must be set out in writing by virtue of ss 60 and 61 of the 1974 Act and comply with the detailed requirements of the Consumer Credit (Agreements) Regulations 1983 (SI 1983/1553). A "consumer hire agreement" is defined as "an agreement made by a person with an individual (the 'hirer') for the . . . hiring of goods to the hirer, being an agreement which— (a) is not a hire-purchase agreement, and (b) is capable of subsisting for more than three months". Provided the lessee is not a body corporate, there is no requirement that an individual lessee must be a "consumer". Hence, the lessee may indeed be a businessperson and the contract a commercial contract of hire. Moreover, where the contract of hire falls within the definition of a consumer hire agreement, the 1974 Act imposes various restrictions on the advertising and canvassing of such hirings by lessors. The lessee also enjoys the other protections contained in the 1974 Act: for example, the restricted rights to cancel the agreement in ss 67–73.

UCTA or CRA controls

A non-consumer contract of hire will also be regulated by the Unfair Contract Terms Act 1977 ("UCTA") insofar as the lessor or lessee purports to exclude or restrict liability in respect of a breach of the common-law implied terms. Section 15(2)(a) of UCTA expressly provides so. Thus, clauses excluding liability for breach of duty in the course of a business arising from a common-law implied term will be subject to the "fairness and reasonableness" test by virtue of s 16 of UCTA.

In a situation where a consumer enters a contract of hire with a trader, it is possible for the Consumer Rights Act 2015 to regulate unfair terms. It can also be noted that it is not possible to amend implied terms about the trader's duties to the detriment of the consumer (CRA s 31). Any other contractual term about something that is not so ringfenced would be subject to the usual CRA s 62 assessment of whether it is unfair.

Supply of Goods and Services Act 1982

Sections 11G–11L of the 1982 Act are the relevant sections which apply to non-consumer contracts of hire and reflect the implied terms which apply to non-consumer contracts for the sale of goods and non-consumer contracts of hire-purchase. Section 11L of the 1982 Act stipulates that where the 1982 Act is applicable and it is not excluded in the contract of hire, the *G M Shepherd* case (noted above) does not apply and the common-law implied terms are supplemented but are not overridden or repealed.

Lessor's right to transfer possession

Section 11H of the 1982 Act provides that there is an implied term which gives the lessor the right to transfer possession of the goods to the lessee by way of hire for the period of the hire.

Lessee's right to enjoy quiet possession

Second, the lessee is entitled to enjoy quiet possession of the goods for the period of hire. However, there is an exception so that possession may be disturbed by the owner (for example, where the contract of hire between the lessor and lessee is a sub-lease and the lessor is not the owner of the goods) or some other person entitled to the benefit of any charge or encumbrance disclosed or known to the lessee before the contract is made.

Lessor's duty to ensure goods correspond to description

Where the lessee hires goods from the lessor by description, s 11I of the 1982 Act stipulates that there is an implied term that the goods will correspond to the description. Section 11I(4) of the 1982 Act directs that a contract may amount to a contract of hire of goods corresponding to description where the goods are selected by the lessee.

Lessor's duty to ensure goods correspond to sample

Section 11K states that where the lessor hires or agrees to hire the goods by reference to a sample, there is an implied term that (1) the bulk will correspond with the sample in quality, (2) the lessee will have a reasonable opportunity of comparing the bulk with the sample, and (3) the goods will be free from any defect, making their quality unsatisfactory, which would not be apparent on reasonable examination of the sample.

Lessor's "satisfactory quality" duty

Section 11J of the 1982 Act deals with the quality and fitness for purpose of the goods hired to the lessee. It is stipulated that where goods are supplied by the lessor to the lessee in the course of the lessor's business, there is an implied term that the goods supplied under that contract are of satisfactory quality. Thus, private hires are excluded. The test for determining whether goods are of satisfactory quality is specified in s 11J(3) of the 1982 Act. It is provided that goods are deemed to be of satisfactory quality where they meet the standard that a reasonable person would regard as satisfactory, taking account of any description of the goods, the consideration for the hire (if relevant) and all the other relevant circumstances.

Lessor's "fitness for purpose" duty

Section 11J(5) and (6) of the 1982 Act set out the "fitness for purpose" implied term. Thus, where the lessor hires goods in the course of a business to the lessee and the lessee, expressly or by implication, makes known to the lessor in the course of negotiations conducted by them in relation to the making of the contract any particular purpose for which the goods are being hired, there is an implied term that the goods supplied under the contract are reasonably fit for that purpose, whether or not that is a purpose for which such goods are commonly supplied. However, the "fitness for purpose" implied term is inapplicable where the lessee does not rely, or it is unreasonable for the lessee to rely, on the skill or judgement of the lessor.

Disapplication of statutory implied terms

Section 11L of the 1982 Act stipulates that where a right, duty or liability would arise under an implied term of the contract of hire, it may be excluded or varied by the parties by express agreement or by a course of dealing between them, or by such usage as binds both parties to the contract of hire. An express term is deemed to exclude or vary an implied term where it is deemed to be inconsistent with that implied term. Needless to say, these provisions which permit the contracting out of implied terms are subject to the statutory constraints on exclusion and limitation of liability clauses contained in UCTA and so may be susceptible to review in terms of the "fair and reasonable" test contained therein.

Essential Facts

- There are a number of modern forms of the contract of hire, including the finance lease, the operating lease, the contract hire and the rental or hire agreement.
- There are four essential elements to the contract of hire, namely a thing to be let, a rent, the consent of the contracting parties and a specified period of let.

- The common law and (in a non-consumer context) the Supply of Goods and Services Act 1982 imply various terms into the contract of hire.
- Those implied terms impose obligations on the lessor and the lessee.

Essential Cases

Wilson v Orr (1879): although the rent should be in money, rather than money's worth, the Court of Session was prepared to classify as a contract of hire the hire of a horse in return for a rent consisting of providing the horse's keep.

Wilson v Norris (1810): there is a common-law implied term that the lessor is under a duty to deliver the subjects of hire to the lessee in a state of good condition and repair.

G M Shepherd Ltd v North West Securities Ltd (1991): in the case of a finance lease or an operating lease where the lessor is not involved in the selection of the hired goods, the contract will be treated as a sui generis contract (ie not as a contract of hire) and so the implied term that the lessor has a good unencumbered title to the goods will not apply.

Seton v Paterson (1880): where a horse was hired for the purpose of undertaking a day's journey, but was taken for a gallop race by the lessee, the lessee was held to be in breach of the implied term to use the horse for the purpose for which it was let.

Campbell v Lord Kennedy (1828): the lessee of a horse was deemed to be in breach of the implied term to take proper care of the goods hired where he lent the horse to a friend whose actions resulted in the horse catching a chill and dying.

3 AGENCY

Businesses often engage agents to act on their behalf as intermediaries to sell their products or services. The reasons for engaging an agent range from lack of time and lack of expertise to lack of knowledge of a particular marketplace. The law of agency regulates the relationship among a principal, an agent and a third party. The principal is the person on whose behalf the agent acts; the agent is the party who has power to act as an intermediary on behalf of the principal; and the third party is the party who enters into a contract with the principal through the agent.

In this chapter, the law of agency will be analysed in detail. First, the different types of agency and the constitution of the agency relationship will be considered. Second, the nature of an agent's authority to bind the principal in contract or otherwise and the rights and obligations of each of the parties to the agency relationship will be explored. Finally, consideration will be given to the termination of the agency relationship and the implications of termination.

SOURCES OF AGENCY LAW

The common law is the main source of the law of agency. However, the Commercial Agents (Council Directive) Regulations 1993 (SI 1993/3053) ("the Regulations") contain a number of special rules which apply to some agency relationships.

DEFINITION OF AGENT AND TYPES OF AGENT

No strict legal definition of an agent has been approved by the courts in Scotland. Professor Sir T B Smith submitted the following definition of agency, which, while useful, is technically not wholly comprehensive:

> "a person who has authority to act for and on behalf of another (called the principal) in contracting legal relations with third parties; and the agent representing the principal creates, alters, or discharges legal obligations of a contractual nature between the latter and third parties".

Thus, the agency relationship is tripartite, envisaging a principal, an agent and a third party. The agent will be paid a fee in respect of their expertise in the local market over which the agent has been appointed and will usually have the power to bind the principal contractually with third parties. However, as stated, the above definition is under-inclusive. For example, the Regulations provide their own definition of a commercial agent which is distinct from the above definition. Regulation 2(1) of the Regulations provides that a commercial agent is a self-employed intermediary who has continuing authority to negotiate the sale or purchase of goods on behalf of their principal, or to negotiate and conclude the sale or purchase of goods on behalf of and in the name of that principal.

General and special agents

Agents may be classified into distinct groupings which highlight the nature of the (implied) authority to bind the principal which they enjoy and also commonly serve to outline the nature of the agent's relationship with the principal or third parties. For example, a general agent is understood to be an agent who is engaged to carry out any or all of the business of a principal. While the matter is not free from doubt (see Bell's *Principles*, s 219(7)), it appears to be the case that a solicitor will be a general agent. Meanwhile, a special agent is an agent who is authorised to carry out one specific particular transaction or a series of identifiable transactions (for example, *Morrison* v *Statter* (1885)). Brief mention should also be made of the uncommon situation of *del credere* agents, where the agent effectively acts as cautioner to guarantee performance of the principal.

CONSTITUTION OF AGENCY

There cannot be an agent without there being a principal (consider *McMeekin* v *Easton* (1889) and *Halifax Life Ltd* v *DLA Piper Scotland Ltd* (2009)). An agency relationship does not require to be created in writing and an oral agency is valid. However, where the relationship between an agent and a principal is one of commercial agency in terms of reg 2(1) of the Regulations, reg 13 of the Regulations confers upon a party the right to call on the other to produce a written signed document setting out the terms of the agency contract including any terms subsequently agreed. An agency may be created by conduct where the agent commences acting on behalf of a principal. The effect of that rule is that the agency relationship may be constituted expressly (ie in writing or orally) or impliedly (ie by conduct) but a court will ordinarily require clear evidence before agency will be inferred (see, for example, *Batt Cables plc* v *Spencer Business Parks Ltd* (2010)). Another form of agency, known as *negotiorum gestio*, arises by operation of law where the administration of the affairs of one person is conducted of necessity by a person in a situation of benevolent intervention who is deemed to be an agent. Here, there is no requirement for offer and acceptance and the agency relationship is created by necessity (see, for example, *Fernie* v *Robertson* (1871)). Finally, an agency relationship may be constituted in the absence of offer and acceptance by ratification by the principal. Such ratification will be relevant where a person, without the prior authority of the principal, purports to bind the principal in contract with a third party and the principal elects to ratify the actions of that person retrospectively.

THE AGENT'S AUTHORITY

Express and implied authority

An agent's authority may be express, implied or ostensible/apparent. One of the objectives of the rules on authority is to protect third parties. Express authority arises where the principal has specifically given the agent authority to enter into particular transactions on its behalf or to engage in certain conduct on its behalf. Usually, such authority will be conferred in a written agreement entered into between the agent and the principal or orally. An agent may also have implied authority by virtue of the nature of their agency. For example, a general agent will have the authority to carry out any or all of the business of the principal. However, not so in the case of a special agent. Likewise, a mercantile agent in the context of the Factors Act 1889 will have implied authority to sell or buy the goods of the principal.

Ostensible/apparent authority

In the case of ostensible/apparent authority, an agent exceeds their authority. Nevertheless, provided certain criteria are satisfied, the third party with whom the agent has dealt will be protected from the unauthorised agent's actions and the principal will be bound by the contract concluded by the agent and liable to the third party on the contract. Where the doctrine of apparent/ostensible authority applies, the principal is precluded from denying the agent's authority to the third party or to act inconsistently so as to give the third party conflicting messages (consider, for example, *International Sponge Importers Ltd* v *Watt & Sons* (1911)). For that reason, ostensible/apparent authority is an example of personal bar on the part of the principal.

Criteria for establishment of ostensible/apparent authority

The leading authority which defines the main criteria for the establishment of ostensible/apparent authority is the English case of *Freeman & Lockyer* v *Buckhurst Park Properties (Mangal) Ltd* (1964), which was approved by Lord President Hope in the Inner House of the Court of Session in *Dornier GmbH* v *Cannon* (1991). Thus, ostensible/apparent authority necessitates the existence of each of the following elements:

- a legal relationship between the principal and the third-party contractor created by a representation made by the principal to the third-party contractor;

- that representation must have been intended to be and in fact must have been acted on by the third-party contractor;

- that representation must have been to the effect that the agent has the authority to enter on behalf of the principal into a contract of a kind within the scope of the agent's apparent authority in such terms to render the principal liable to perform any obligations imposed on them by such a contract.

Key criteria

With regard to the first criterion, it is crucial that the principal represents to the third party that the agent does not lack authority. This may be in writing, orally or by positive or negative conduct, ie the principal's actions or omissions (*Freeman & Lockyer* v *Buckhurst Park Properties (Mangal) Ltd* (1964)). The third party must also demonstrate that it relied on the principal's representation and that loss was sustained as a result of such reliance. Moreover, the third party is under an obligation to show that the conduct of the principal caused it to believe that the agent had authority to enter into the contract. The result of the latter rule is that if the third party has knowledge from another source that the agent is exceeding their authority, it will be impossible for the third party to establish a causal link between the principal's actions or omissions and the third party's "belief" that the agent has authorisation. Accordingly, the third party will be unable to obtain the benefit of the doctrine of ostensible/apparent authority (*Colvin* v *Dixon* (1867)).

Alternative means for the creation of ostensible authority

Ostensible/apparent authority may be created through a course of dealing. For example, where an agent at one point had general authority to carry out all of the business of the principal (and so is a general agent), but the principal then terminates the agent's general authority without notifying third-party contractors, ostensible/apparent authority may arise in respect of a third party who deals regularly with that agent. Of course, if the third party becomes aware through one source or another that the agent's

authority has come to an end, that third party will be precluded from rely-
ing on the doctrine of ostensible/apparent authority (*North of Scotland Banking Corp* v *Behn, Moller & Co* (1881)). The counsel of perfection is for the
principal to make it clear to third-party customers that the authority of the
agent has ceased, through either correspondence or general advertisements.
A good example of that process is set out in the case of partners as agents in
s 36 of the Partnership Act 1890.

Effect of ostensible authority

In circumstances where the third party is able to establish each of these
criteria, it is important to stress that the effect of the establishment of osten-
sible/apparent authority is not to validate the contract or to cure the agent's
lack of authority. The contract remains invalid and the agent remains unauthorised. However, the effect is that the principal is personally barred from
claiming that the agent lacked authority in any action raised by the third
party against the principal based on the contract: for example, an action for
the recovery of damages for the loss sustained by the third party in respect
of a breach of the principal's obligations under the contract.

Ratification

Where the agent has exceeded their authority and none of the rules on
express, implied or ostensible/apparent authority operates to cure the position, then if the agent has purported to bind the principal in contract, the
general rule is that the principal will not be bound. However, provided
certain criteria are fulfilled, the principal may unilaterally ratify (expressly,
impliedly or from its actions or omissions) the agent's conduct. The principal's ratification may relate to either an existing agent's lack of authority or
a person who is not actually an agent of the principal. In this latter scenario
the ratifying conduct of the principal operates to create an agency relationship where none had existed before (*Alexander Ward & Co Ltd* v *Samyang
Navigation Co Ltd* (1975)). Ratification functions in a retrospective manner
whereby a contractual relationship is deemed to have existed between the
principal and a third-party contractor from the moment that the agent purported to bind the principal.

Criteria for ratification

There are certain prerequisites which must be satisfied for valid ratification
to operate. First, there must be a principal in existence at the point at which
the agent (who lacks the necessary authority) purports to bind the principal
in contract with a third party. If the principal did not exist at that point in

time, the principal has no power to ratify and so the agent may find themselves personally liable on the contract with the third party. This criterion is particularly important where the principal is a body corporate and is not incorporated when the agent seeks to bind it in contract with the third party (see s 51(1) of the Companies Act 2006). Second, if the principal does exist at that time, it must also have legal capacity at that time and also when it purports to ratify the agent's actions (*Boston Deep Sea Fishing and Ice Co Ltd v Farnham* (1957)). Thus, if the contract between the principal and the third party is beyond the statutory powers of the principal, that is *ultra vires* (for example in the case of a public body), ratification will be impossible. Third, the contract must not be void or illegal. Fourth, if it is alleged that the principal unilaterally ratified the agent's actions by its actions or omissions, there must be evidence to enable an inference to be drawn that the principal was fully briefed of all relevant facts. Thus, if there is some gap or error in the principal's knowledge regarding the actions of the agent, there will be evidence that the principal was not fully aware of all relevant facts and that its purported ratification was defective. Fifth, there must be evidence to demonstrate that the agent entered into the transaction with the third party as an agent. For example, in circumstances where a person enters into a contract with a third party on their own account, there would be insufficient evidence to enable a principal to ratify the actions of that person to create an agency relationship afresh. The rationale for that rule is that the "agent" did not actually enter into the agreement with the third party on behalf of the principal, but instead for their own personal purposes. Thus, ratification is precluded (*Keighley, Maxsted & Co v Durant* (1901)). Sixth, there is a rule to the effect that the principal must ratify within a specified time limit where the actions of the agent which require to be ratified are subject to such a time limit (*Goodall v Bilsland* (1909)). Finally, there is now a rule which mirrors English law to the effect that ratification will be precluded where it results in unfair prejudice to the interests of third parties (*Gray v Baird Logistics (UK) Ltd* (2017), drawing on *The Borvigilant* (2003)). This means that if circumstances arise where the effect of the ratification is detrimental to the interests of the third party, ratification cannot operate to confer legal validity.

THE DUTIES OF THE AGENT AND THE RIGHTS OF THE PRINCIPAL

Duties of the agent

The agent's duties may be divided into non-fiduciary duties and fiduciary duties. The first non-fiduciary duty imposes an obligation on the agent to follow the principal's instructions. If the principal's instructions are unclear, the agent is not liable. Regulation 3(2)(c) of the Regulations imposes an obligation on a commercial agent to comply with reasonable instructions given by the principal. In terms of *Gilmour* v *Clark* (1853), if the agent breaches the instructions of the principal, he is liable in damages for any loss suffered by the principal. Second, the agent must exercise skill and care in performing their obligations. The standard of care is based on a mixture of objective and subjective tests. Thus, if the agent is a qualified chartered accountant, their subjective qualities and skills will operate to lift the objective standard of care so that their duty will be that of a reasonably competent and careful member of the accountancy profession. Where the agent fails to meet the relevant standard of care and so breaches their duty, they will be liable to the principal in damages. The final non-fiduciary duty of the agent is to keep accounts in writing or in some other more informal medium, depending on what has been agreed between the agent and the principal.

Introduction to fiduciary duties

The law recognises that the relationship between the agent and the principal is one of mutual trust and good faith. Thus, the principal duty is for the agent to act in good faith and disclose all facts and circumstances with regard to the principal's business (Bell's *Principles*, s 222). One case noted that an agent must act "100%, body and soul" for the principal (*Imageview Management Ltd* v *Jack* (2009)), although it might be noted that an agent with very limited authority might not be subject to extensive fiduciary duties. Regulation 3(1) of the Regulations builds on the common-law duty of good faith by providing that all commercial agents must look after the interests of their principals and act dutifully and in good faith. In terms of reg 3(2) of the Regulations, this includes the agent (1) making proper efforts to negotiate and, where appropriate, concluding the transactions they are instructed to take care of, (2) communicating to the principal all the necessary information available to them, and (3) complying with reasonable instructions given by the principal.

The fiduciary duties

The first fiduciary duty to consider is the agent's duty to account to the principal in respect of all benefits received in connection with the principal's business. Sums generated in the course of the agency business must be accounted for, for example commissions and other sums in money or money's worth. An agent cannot take commission without knowledge and consent of the principal (*Commonwealth Oil and Gas Co Ltd* v *Baxter* (2010)).

However, in terms of *Lothian* v *Jenolite Ltd* (1969), an agent does not require
to account for extra income they have generated by working for a com-
petitor of the principal in the absence of a non-competition restrictive cov-
enant. Where the agent breaches this fiduciary duty, the remedy is an action
of accounting rather than damages: that is, the gain enjoyed by the agent
may be disgorged and transferred to the principal. However, if the agent has
not enjoyed any gain, the principal's action will be incompetent (*Sao Paolo
Alpargatas SA* v *Standard Chartered Bank Ltd* (1985)).

Second, there is a fiduciary duty to the effect that the agent must not
disclose or exploit confidential information regarding the business of the
principal. Third, a duty is imposed to the effect that the agent is disentitled from entering into transactions whereby the agent generates a profit
at the principal's expense – the so-called "no-profit" rule (*Cunningham*
v *Lee* (1874)). Fourth, the agent may not delegate their duties to a third
party, subject to certain exceptions. Those exceptions reflect the fact that
the agent has been specifically chosen to perform by the principal, that is
delectus personae applies. Finally, there is a duty to relieve the principal of any
liability suffered as a result of the agent entering into any contract in excess
of authority – see *Milne* v *Ritchie* (1882).

THE DUTIES OF THE PRINCIPAL AND THE RIGHTS OF THE AGENT

Principal's duties

Where the agency is a commercial agency, reg 4(1) of the Regulations
stipulates that the principal must act dutifully and in good faith towards the
commercial agent. In particular, the principal must provide the commercial
agent with the necessary documentation relating to the goods concerned
and obtain for the commercial agent the information necessary for the performance of the agency contract, and in particular notify the agent within a
reasonable period once he anticipates that the volume of commercial transactions will be significantly lower than that which the commercial agent
could normally have expected. Moreover, the principal is under an obligation to inform the agent within a reasonable period of their acceptance or
refusal of, and of any non-execution by them of, a commercial transaction
which the commercial agent has procured for them.

The agent's rights: payment

Mackersy's Executors v *St Giles Cathedral Managing Board* (1904) directs that
there is a presumption that the agent is entitled to be paid for services

rendered where the agency represents their livelihood. Of course, usually an express term is included in a written agency agreement setting out the remuneration of the agent, including whether they are to be paid a flat fee or commission on sales generated. The common law provides that commission will be payable in the event that the transaction was concluded as a result of the actings of the agent or the agent's actions materially contributed to the same (*Walker, Fraser & Steele* v *Fraser's Trustees* (1910)). Where the agent is a commercial agent and the agreement entered into between the agent and the principal does not stipulate the agent's payment terms, reg 6 of the Regulations assumes importance. Here, it is provided that the commercial agent is entitled to the remuneration that commercial agents appointed for the goods forming the subject of the agency contract are customarily allowed in the place where the agent carries on their activities. If there is no such customary practice, a commercial agent is entitled to reasonable remuneration taking into account all the aspects of the transaction. Regulations 7 and 8 also provide for the payment of commission to the commercial agent on commercial transactions during the period covered by the agency contract and beyond.

The agent's rights: reimbursement of expenses and lien

An agent has the right to be reimbursed in respect of all expenses incurred in the proper performance of their duties. This right is accompanied by a right of relief relative to all liabilities sustained by the agent in the proper performance of their duties. Finally, the agent enjoys a right of lien over the goods of the principal in security for payment of commission or other remuneration.

THIRD-PARTY CONTRACTS

Where third parties enter into contracts with the principal through the intervention of the agent, the general rule is that the agent does not become contractually bound to the third party despite the fact that he has undertaken the work in ensuring the conclusion of such a contract. Where an agent discloses that they are an agent, the effect on contractual relations between the principal and the third party depends on the nature of the agent's communication with the third party regarding the existence and identity of the principal. The legal position is best analysed by categorising circumstances into three elements:

(1) where the agent discloses that they are an agent, that there is a principal and they identify the principal;

(2) where the agent discloses that they are an agent, that there is a principal but they fail to name and identify the principal; and

(3) where the agent fails to inform the third party that there was a principal on whose behalf they were acting.

Scenario 1

Here, the principal will be bound into a contract with the third party and the agent will incur no personal liability (*Stone and Rolfe Ltd* v *Kimber Coal Co Ltd* (1926)). *Armour* v *T L Duff & Co* (1912) ruled that the position will be the same where the principal is not specifically named but the principal can be identified with little effort. However, in certain contexts it is either customary or standard practice for agents specifically to incur personal liability on a contract entered into between the principal and the third party: for example, when solicitors enter into letters of obligation in respect of transactions involving the conveyance of heritable property by their clients (albeit such letters are less common than they once were following the reform of land registration law that came into force in 2014).

Scenario 2

Here, the Scots law position is not particularly clear. In certain circumstances, it will be possible for the court to identify the principal and, here, the agent will bear no personal liability. However, where it is not possible to ascertain the name of the principal from the surrounding circumstances, then the third party has a choice: the third party may elect to hold the principal or the agent personally liable on the contract in terms of the cases of *Lamont Nisbett & Co* v *Hamilton* (1907) and *Ferrier* v *Dods* (1865). However, if the agent declines to name the principal when asked to do so, the agent will incur personal liability (*Gibb* v *Cunningham and Robertson* (1925)).

Scenario 3

Where the agent fails to disclose the existence of a principal, the general rule is that the agent incurs liability to the third party with whom he contracts unless the third party, on learning of the existence of the principal, elects to hold the principal liable. Moreover, an agent for an undisclosed principal will be personally liable in damages for personal injuries sustained by a third party where the latter is working on the premises of the undisclosed principal (*Ruddy* v *Monte Marco* (2008)). However, the liability is not alternative: the third party cannot choose to sue both the principal and agent and must hold one liable or the other (*Bennett* v *Inveresk Paper Co* (1891)). Yet there are circumstances where a written contract is concluded between the agent and the third party and it is impossible as a matter of implication or interpretation for the third party to elect to hold that the principal is liable.

Ratification in context of undisclosed principal

In circumstances where a principal fails to ratify the actions of an agent who has exceeded their authority, the agent may or may not be personally liable on the contract with the third party. Bell, *Commentaries*, I, 543 directs that it is not always the case that the agent will be personally bound and in circumstances where the agent is not so personally liable to the third party, it may be the case that no contract subsists between the agent and the third party at all. Whatever the position, what is certain is that no contract will arise between the principal and the third party.

An alternative scenario

To the three categories and scenarios of the third party's knowledge of the agency situation discussed above, a fourth category may be added, although on a proper analysis it is not really a category at all. Where there is no principal whatsoever, perhaps in a situation where a corporate entity does not exist, the purported agent will not necessarily enter into a direct contractual relationship with the counterparty. That being the case, it would still be inadvisable to act in such a manner, as the counterparty may raise an action against the purported agent on the basis of a breach of warranty of authority (*Halifax Life Ltd* v *DLA Piper Scotland Ltd* (2009), with reference to *Scott* v *J B Livingston & Nicol* (1990)). It can also be noted that s 51 of the Companies Act 2006 operates to personally bind the promoters of a company who purport to enter into a contract on behalf of a company prior to its incorporation.

TERMINATION OF THE AGENCY CONTRACT

Common-law termination

A distinction requires to be made between termination of the agency contract at common law and termination of a commercial agency contract. First, with regard to common-law termination, it is recognised that the agency contract may end with the expiry of a fixed-term contract, by mutual agreement or in circumstances where the objective of the agency relationship has ended (*Rhodes* v *Forwood* (1875)). It is also understood that the principal or agent may unilaterally revoke the agency relationship unless there is an express term to the contrary in the agency contract. Where one of the parties elects unilaterally to revoke, Erskine, *Institute*, III, 3, 40 stipulates that that person may be liable in damages in respect of losses incurred by the other party as a result of early termination (*Turner* v *Goldsmith* (1891)). The mental incapacity of the agent will put an end to the agent's authority (*Drew* v *Nunn* (1878)). Finally, since the law treats the agency relationship as one involving *delectus personae*, the death of the agent or principal automatically terminates the agency contract.

Termination of commercial agency: notice periods

In the case of a commercial agency, the provisions concerning the periods of notice of termination in the Regulations will demand consideration. It is provided in reg 15(2)(a), (b) and (c) of the Regulations that either party seeking to terminate the agency contract must give a minimum of 1 month's notice to the other in the first year of the agency contract, 2 months' notice to the other in the second year and 3 months' notice where the contract has endured for 3 years or more. Since these are minimum periods of notice, it is possible for the agency contract to stipulate longer periods.

Termination of commercial agency: payment of compensation or indemnity

On termination, an agent has the right to be paid compensation or indemnity. Regulation 19 of the Regulations directs that any provision of an agency contract which purports to exclude the agent's right to be paid compensation or indemnity is void. In the absence of provision in the agency contract stipulating for indemnity, reg 17(2) of the Regulations states that the commercial agent is entitled to compensation. Regulation 17(9) narrates that if the commercial agent fails to notify the principal within 1 year following the termination of the agency contract that they intend to pursue their entitlement for compensation or indemnity, then their claim becomes time barred. Regulation 18 goes on to list a series of situations where the agent's right to be paid compensation or indemnity on termination is expressly excluded: first, where the principal terminates the agency contract due to a breach or default which has been caused by frustration of the agency contract; and, second, where the agent has terminated the agency contract. However, there are exceptions to this general rule: first, where the agent's actions in terminating the agency contract are attributable to the principal's breach of contract; and, second, the agent has a right to be paid compensation or indemnity where they were justified in terminating the agency contract on the grounds of age, infirmity or serious illness.

Indemnity

From a principal's perspective, it will usually be the case that the payment of an indemnity is preferable over the payment of compensation, since the sums payable to the agent in terms of an indemnity are capped at 1 year's commission duly calculated on the basis of the average of the last 5 years of the agency or, if the agency has endured for a shorter period, the annual average over the period of the agency. This can be contrasted with the sums payable to the agent in terms of compensation, which are open ended. The purpose of the indemnity payment is to enable the agent to gain some advantage from the increase in the principal's business which has been generated as a result of their activities (reg 17(3)). The grant of an indemnity does not preclude the agent from seeking damages.

Compensation

Regulation 17(6) of the Regulations specifically provides that the objective of compensation is to compensate the agent for the damage suffered as a result of the premature termination of the agency relationship. Regulation 17(7) sets out further details of how such damage is calculated to the effect that it is deemed to occur particularly when the termination takes place in either or both of the following circumstances, namely circumstances which (a) deprive the commercial agent of the commission which proper performance of the agency contract would have procured for them while providing their principal with substantial benefits linked to the activities of the commercial agent, or (b) have not enabled the commercial agent to amortise the costs and expenses that they had incurred in the performance of the agency contract on the advice of their principal.

The approach of the courts towards the calculation of compensation was dealt with by the Scottish courts in *King* v *T Tunnock Ltd* (2000) and by the House of Lords on an appeal from an English case in *Lonsdale* v *Howard & Hallam Ltd* (2007). In *King*, it was held that the mode of calculation of compensation deployed by French law which awards 2 years' loss of average gross commission ought to be applied (in the instant case Mr King had been engaged as a commercial agent for Tunnocks for approximately 32 years when his agency contract was terminated). However, in *Lonsdale*, Lord Hoffmann in the House of Lords declined to follow the French model of awarding 2 years' loss of average gross commission and ruled that the courts enjoy discretion in fixing the level of compensation. Lord Hoffmann took the view that this approach would be fortified in a case such as *Lonsdale*, where the business of the principal was in prolonged decline. His Lordship was of the view that the better way of analysing the calculation of compensation was to understand that the agent was being compelled to hand back the goodwill of the principal's business which the agent had been involved in creating at the point of termination.

Essential Facts

- The Scots law of agency is regulated by the common law and the Commercial Agents (Council Directive) Regulations 1993.
- The law of agency regulates the relationship which arises among a principal, an agent and a third party.
- The principal is the person on whose behalf the agent acts; the agent is the party who has power to act as an intermediary on behalf of the principal; and the third party is the party who enters into a contract with the principal through the agent.
- Agents may be special or general, which is descriptive of the authority which that agent wields.
- An agency relationship does not require to be created in writing and an oral agency is valid.
- An agent's authority may be express, implied or ostensible/apparent.
- Express authority arises where the principal has specifically given the agent authority to enter into particular transactions on its behalf or to engage in certain conduct on its behalf.
- An agent may have implied authority by virtue of the nature of the agency: for example, a general agent will have the authority to carry out any or all of the business of the principal.
- Ostensible/apparent authority arises where a representation is made by the principal to a third party that the agent has the authority to enter on behalf of the principal into a contract of a kind within the scope of the agent's authority.
- Where an agent exceeds their authority, in certain circumstances, the principal may ratify the agent's conduct.
- The agent's duties may be divided into fiduciary and non-fiduciary duties.
- The agent has a right to be remunerated, a right to recover expenses, a right of lien and, in the case of a commercial agency, the principal must act dutifully and in good faith towards the commercial agent.
- The extent of an agent's liability to a third party on a contract depends on whether the agent: (1) discloses that they are an agent, (2) discloses that there is a principal, and/or (3) identifies a principal.

- At common law, the agency contract may be determined by the expiry of a fixed-term contract, by mutual agreement or in circumstances where the objective of the agency relationship has ended. The principal or agent may unilaterally revoke the agency relationship unless there is an express term to the contrary in the agency contract; and the death of the agent or principal automatically terminates the agency contract.
- Where a commercial agency is terminated by the principal, the agent will be entitled to be paid compensation or an indemnity.

Essential Cases

Morrison v Statter (1885): distinguishes a special agent from a general agent.

Freeman & Lockyer v Buckhurst Park Properties (Mangal) Ltd (1964): articulates the three elements for the establishment of ostensible/apparent authority.

Keighley, Maxsted & Co v Durant (1901): one of the prerequisites of ratification is that the agent must have entered into the transaction with the third party as an agent.

Gilmour v Clark (1853): if the agent breaches the principal's instructions, he is liable in damages for any loss suffered by the principal.

Cunningham v Lee (1874): the agent is under a fiduciary duty not to enter into transactions whereby the agent generates a profit at the principal's expense – the so-called "no-profit" rule.

Milne v Ritchie (1882): an agent is under a fiduciary duty to relieve the principal of any liability suffered as a result of the agent entering into any contract in excess of authority.

Mackersy's Executors v St Giles Cathedral Managing Board (1904): there is a common-law presumption that the agent is entitled to be paid for services rendered where the agency represents their livelihood.

Walker, Fraser & Steele v Fraser's Trustees (1910): the common law provides that commission will be payable to the agent where a transaction was concluded as a result of the actings of the agent or the agent's actions materially contributed to the same.

Lonsdale v Howard & Hallam Ltd (2007): on the termination of a commercial agency, the agent should be compensated in respect of the goodwill of the principal's business which he is being asked to hand back to the principal at the point of termination and which he had been actively involved in creating during the subsistence of the agency relationship.

4   INSURANCE

Insurance is an important commercial activity in the UK. Since the inception of the insurance market, the law has recognised the need to regulate its operation. The law achieves this through a mixture of common law and statutory regulation. As we shall see, legislation is now particularly important in this sphere, owing in particular to the Consumer Insurance (Disclosure and Representations) Act 2012 ("CIDRA") and the Insurance Act 2015. Older statutes may also be of relevance (such as the Life Assurance Act 1774 and the Marine Insurance Act 1906).

PURPOSE OF INSURANCE

The objective of an insured in entering into an insurance contract is to protect the insured against the occurrence of a particular misfortune or particular risks: for example, motor insurance protects the insured in the event that the insured's vehicle is damaged or destroyed. The nature of that protection (ie whether the insured has a right of repair or a right to be paid compensation for loss) is regulated by the terms of the insurance contract. However, the crucial point is that in some way the insured will be safeguarded in the event that the perils or risks described in the insurance contract occur.

THE NATURE OF INSURANCE

There are essentially two types of insurance. First, there is indemnity insurance, which entitles the insured to indemnification from the insurer on the occurrence of an event or a peril specified in the insurance contract (for example, theft of property, fire, or damage to a building and its contents insurance). The second form of insurance is life assurance. In the case of indemnity insurance, the peril is uncertain to occur, whereas, in the case of life assurance, it is certain that the life insured will come to an end at some point in time. For clarity, the word "assurance" tends to be used in place of "insurance" in the context of arrangements for cover in relation to a person's death, as witnessed in the terminology of the Life Assurance Act 1774.

DEFINITION OF INSURANCE

There have been many attempts by the courts in Scotland and England to define an insurance contract. None has been completely satisfactory. Statutory definitions have been eschewed by the legislature. A close approximation to a definition is contained in the case of *Prudential Insurance Co* v *Inland Revenue Commissioners* (1904). In terms of the *Prudential* definition, there are four elements which must be satisfied, as follows:

(1) consideration must pass from the insured to the insurer (which is a periodical payment called the premium);
(2) the insured must secure a benefit, usually the payment of a sum of money;
(3) upon the happening of some event;
(4) which involves an element of uncertainty as to (a) whether the event will happen or not, or (b) the time at which it will happen.

Furthermore, the event referred to in (3) must be adverse to the interests of the insured (*Department of Trade and Industry* v *St Christopher's Motorists Association* (1974)).

CONSTITUTION OF CONTRACT OF INSURANCE

An insurance contract does not require to be reduced to writing in order to be legally valid in terms of Scots law. Section 1(1) of the Requirements of Writing (Scotland) Act 1995 provides that writing is not generally required for the constitution of any contract. An insurance contract is not one of the exceptions to this starting point. However, in the context of marine insurance, s 22 of the Marine Insurance Act 1906 provides that a marine policy will not be admissible in court unless it is embodied in written form.

INSURABLE INTEREST

A party to an insurance contract must have insurable interest in the subject-matter of insurance. In examining the nature of the interest which the insured must possess, it is beneficial to make a distinction between life assurance and indemnity insurance policies.

Life assurance

First, in the context of life assurance, s 1 of the Life Assurance Act 1774 states that an insurance policy will be void where a person takes out a life assurance policy over the life of another person in which he has no interest. The nature of that interest is stipulated in s 3 of the Life Assurance Act 1774. Here, the fundamental point is made that the interest must be of a pecuniary or financial variety. For example, a son will have insurable interest in the life of his father due to the son's financial right to the payment of aliment. Likewise, s 1 of the Married Women's Policies of Assurance (Scotland) Act 1880 narrates that a wife has the right to effect a policy of assurance on the life of her husband. In the case of *Dalby* v *India and London Life Assurance Co* (1854), it was ruled by the court that it was sufficient that the insured possessed an insurable interest in the life assured at the date the policy of insurance was effected. It is worthwhile stressing that an insurable interest of a pecuniary or financial interest is not necessarily limited to familial relationships. For example, in the case of *Turnbull & Co* v *Scottish Provident Institution* (1896), it was ruled by the Outer House of the Court of Session that a firm had a direct financial interest, and thus an insurable interest, in the life of its local agent in Iceland.

Indemnity insurance

Second, for the purposes of indemnity insurance, the nature of the insurable interest required was outlined in the landmark case of *Macaura* v *Northern Assurance Co Ltd* (1925). In *Macaura*, the insured was a creditor and sole shareholder of a limited company. The company owned a quantity of timber, much of which was stored on the land of the insured. The timber was insured in the name of the insured, not the name of the company. When the timber was destroyed by fire, the insured made a claim and the insurer resisted liability. The court ruled that the insured had no insurable interest in the timber. Only the company had an insurable interest. The court made the point that it is crucial that the insured has a legal or an equitable interest in the property insured. Otherwise, the contract of insurance will be void for lack of insurable interest. Therefore, even in circumstances where an insured has an expectation of, or stands to sustain a loss as a result of, the destruction or damage of the subject-matter of the insurance contract, this may be insufficient to entitle them to indemnification if they are unable to point to a close legal relationship between them and the property insured. Case law has recognised situations where a non-owner has an insurable interest up to a certain level or to a property's full value, such as tenants who are under an obligation to reinstate a property following its damage or destruction (*Aberdeen Harbour Board* v *Heating Enterprises (Aberdeen) Ltd* (1990)) or those obliged to insure the property against its damage or destruction (*Fehilly* v *General Accident Fire and Life Assurance Co* (1982); *Comlex Ltd (In Liquidation)* v *Allianz Insurers Ltd* (2016)).

Consequences of a lack of insurable interest

In the case of a life assurance policy, the consequences of a lack of insurable interest are clear: s 1 of the Life Assurance Act 1774 stipulates that the policy is "null and void". Meanwhile, in the case of indemnity insurance, the Scots common law provides that it is an essential element of a contract of insurance that there is a subject in which the insured has an interest (*The Laws of Scotland: Stair Memorial Encyclopaedia*, vol 12, para 848, citing Bell's *Principles*, s 457). Hence, without that essential element, the contract is void.

WARRANTIES

A warranty is a fundamental term of an insurance policy. It amounts to a promise made by the insured to the insurer. A simple example of a warranty would be a minimum number of crew on a boat for a voyage at sea. If the insured breaches a warranty then the insurer will be under no duty in respect of any loss occurring, or attributable to something happening, after that breach but before the breach has been remedied (s 10 of the Insurance Act 2015, amending s 33 of the Marine Insurance Act 1906). Any risk arising before the breach is still covered (ie the contract is not treated as void from the outset), as is any risk that arises after steps have been taken so as to no longer be in breach (where remediation is possible). This ability to fix a breach of warranty found in the modern statutory regime moves away from the traditional rule applied in the case of *Bank of Nova Scotia* v *Hellenic Mutual War Risk Association (Bermuda) Ltd (The Good Luck)* (1992), which was to the effect that the insurer was simply discharged from liability under the contract with effect from the date of the breach with no prospect of remediation.

A further reform introduced by the Insurance Act 2015 relates to "terms not relevant to the actual loss". This is to the effect that the insurer is not able to rely on the insured's non-compliance with a term that can be seen to relate to a particular type of loss (or a particular timing of such a loss) to escape liability unless the non-compliance could potentially have had some bearing on the risk of the loss which actually occurred. The example given in the Explanatory Notes to the Insurance Act 2015 relates to a term prescribing the use of certain window locks, which would have no relevance to flood risk were flooding to occur. Similarly, a failure to employ a night watchman would suspend the insurer's liability for losses at night but not for losses during the day.

Types of warranty

In an insurance contract, there are essentially two types of warranty:

- a statement of fact by the insured as to the past or present (a "past/present fact warranty only"); or

- a continuing undertaking that a state of affairs will prevail throughout the duration of the policy, which must be exactly complied with, whether it be material to the risk insured or not (a "continuing/promissory warranty").

It is not always straightforward to ascertain whether a term of the policy amounts to a "past/present fact only warranty" or a "continuing/promissory warranty". It is often a matter of interpretation. For example, in the case of *Hussain* v *Brown* (1996), after some dispute between the insurer and the insured, the Court of Appeal ruled that the following words amounted to a "past/present fact only warranty": "Are the premises fitted with any system of intruder alarm. If yes give name of installing company."

Creating warranties and regulation of "basis of the contract" clauses

When it comes to creating a warranty, no magic or special words are required. Whilst it can be helpful to specifically use appropriate wording, there is no need specifically to stipulate that the term is a warranty, and in the event of ambiguity it will be for a court to decide whether something is a warranty or a simple contractual condition. Until recently, it was common for insurance policies to provide that every term of the policy represented the "basis of the contract", to elevate every term of the policy into a warranty (*Dawsons Ltd* v *Bonnin* (1922)). Such "basis of the contract" clauses are no longer competent in both consumer and non-consumer insurance contracts (under s 6 of the Consumer Insurance (Disclosure and Representations) Act 2012 and s 9 of the Insurance Act 2015 respectively).

GOOD FAITH, DISCLOSURE AND FRAUDULENT CLAIMS

A contract of insurance is traditionally viewed as a contract "*uberrimae fidei*", that is, one "of the utmost good faith" – *Carter* v *Boehm* (1766), *Stewart* v *Morison* (1779), *Hooper* v *Royal London Genral Insurance Co* (1993) and s 17 of the Marine Insurance Act 1906. Whilst this underlying starting point of good faith continues in the modern law, s 14 of the Insurance Act 2015 abolished any rule of law that allowed a party to a contract of insurance to avoid that contract on the ground that the utmost good faith has not been observed. What is of particular importance now are the duties imposed on a (prospective) insured party (i) immediately before the insurance contract is formed, that is, at the negotiation stage and until the contract of insurance is formed; and (ii) at the point of renewal of an insurance contract.

There is also a duty not to make a fraudulent claim on the policy. As for the insurer, it too must consider good faith in certain circumstances, for example to make disclosure to co-insureds, assignees or third-party beneficiaries (*Bank of Nova Scotia* v *Hellenic Mutual War Risk Association (Bermuda) Ltd (The Good Luck)* (1992) and *Banque Financière de la Cité SA* v *Westgate Insurance Co Ltd* (1991)).

Disclosure

For many years, the duty of good faith placed a proposer of an insurance contract under a duty of disclosure of all facts which were material to the risks insured in the insurance policy, and a further duty not to misrepresent material facts. Disclosure duties in insurance contracts have been on a statutory footing since 2013 (for consumers) or 2016 (for non-consumers), under the Consumer Insurance (Disclosure and Representations) Act 2012 ("CIDRA") and the Insurance Act 2015 respectively. "Consumer insurance contracts" are defined in s 1 of CIDRA as contracts between an individual entering a contract for purposes unrelated to that individual's trade, business or profession with a person carrying on the business of insurance, whereas non-consumer insurance contracts are simply those insurance contracts not caught by that definition (s 1 of the Insurance Act 2015). As discussed below, the standards of disclosure are slightly different, with consumers being under a reactive duty not to mislead the insurer in their responses to any questions, and non-consumers facing a proactive duty to set out the nature of the risk. The potential consequences of a breach of the relevant duty are set out in the relevant statute, in similar but subtly different terms. As a consumer protection measure, it is not possible to contract out of the consumer protection regime (s 10 CIDRA). There is slightly more scope to contractually vary the situation in non-consumer arrangements but only the default rules are included here. These regimes will be considered in turn.

Consumer disclosure

The substance of the consumer disclosure duty is found in s 2 of CIDRA. Section 2(2) provides: "It is the duty of the consumer to take reasonable care not to make a misrepresentation to the insurer." Section 2(3) clarifies a failure by the consumer to confirm or amend earlier information when requested to do so by the insurer is also a breach of the duty should that amount to a misrepresentation. It is accordingly largely for the insurer to ask for information about the prospective insured. Section 3 of CIDRA then sets out when reasonable care is not shown. This is an objective test:

the standard of care is what a reasonable consumer would say to the insurer in view of all "relevant circumstances". Section 3(2) sets out, non-exhaustively, circumstances that may be considered in this exercise, such as how clear an insurer's questions were. It is then provided that the insurer must also take into account any particular characteristics or circumstances of the customer that it knows or ought to know (s 3(4)). There is also a deeming provision that anything a consumer does that is dishonest equates to a lack of reasonable care (s 3(5)).

Consequences of not meeting the disclosure duty There is a statutory scheme that must be followed to work out whether there are any consequences to a breach and, if so, what those consequences are. The first important step in that process involves the concept of the "qualifying misrepresentation" (QM). QMs are relevant when it comes to the remedies of the insurer because, as detailed in section 4, a breach of the duty to take reasonable care to avoid making a misrepresentation might not of itself give a remedy. The insurer is only able to unlock a remedy where the consumer is in breach of the duty in s 2 of CIDRA and the insurer can show that that breach was relevant to whether the insurer would have (a) entered the contract at all, or (b) entered it on different terms.

A further consideration is that there are two different levels of QM, and the level of QM is relevant to which remedy the insurer has access to. Section 5 of CIDRA divides QMs into (a) deliberate or reckless; or (b) careless. A QM is "deliberate or reckless" where, first, there is a knowing untruth (or lack of care about truth) and, second, that was known to be (or no care was taken as to whether it was) relevant to the insurer. An example would be failing to disclose a previous conviction for a road traffic offence when applying for motor insurance after being specifically asked about that by the insurer. Careless QMs constitute all other QMs, that is, they do not measure up to both those requirements. It is for the insurer to establish the deliberate or reckless status of the QM.

The precise remedy for the insurer will then be determined in accordance with Schedule 1 to CIDRA. For a deliberate or reckless QM, the insurer can: avoid the contract, refuse all claims (in all circumstances), and keep the premiums already paid by the consumer (unless premium retention is deemed unfair to the consumer).

The consequences are not so severe for careless QMs, and there is some scope for the insurance arrangement continuing in existence. There are two potential outcomes. If the careless QM induced the insurer to enter the contract, the insurer can avoid the contract and reject any claims but must return the premiums. This situation applies where, but for the careless QM, there would be no contract at all. The alternative is where the careless QM did not induce the formation of the contract, but rather the breach of duty led to a contract which would have been entered into anyway having slightly different parameters. Where this led to different terms from the insurer's norm being applied (other than amount of premium), the remedy is that the normal terms will be deemed to apply to the insurance. If the terms would have otherwise been the same but the price would have been higher, the cover provided is proportionately reduced on the basis of the lower premiums actually paid. There is a formula for this which will be explained below in the non-consumer context. Further, the insurer is also allowed to prospectively terminate (ie not avoid) the contract (unless it is a life assurance policy) on giving reasonable notice. This is the insurer's option, and the insured cannot object to it being exercised. For a life policy, whilst there is no option to terminate, from an insurer's point of view the cover will at least be reduced pro rata or the terms adapted. The net effect of all of this is a contract that was adapted in its terms will revert to the terms that should have applied, and if a consumer enjoyed cheaper premiums then the cover provided will reflect what was paid.

Non-consumer disclosure

Owing to the perceived more equal balance of power between a non-consumer insured and the insurer counterparty, this regime is slightly less generous to the insured than the insurance provisions concerning consumers. A business insured must provide the insurer with a "fair presentation of the risk". This duty, found in Part 2 of the Insurance Act 2015 Act, is more proactive than reactive in nature.

Under s 3 of the Insurance Act 2015, before a contract of insurance is entered into, the insured must make to the insurer a fair presentation of the risk, with subsection (3) providing that a fair presentation of the risk is one which makes the disclosure required by subsection (4) (as explained below) in a manner that is reasonably clear and accessible, is substantially correct in terms of material representations as to matters of fact and every material representation as to a matter of expectation or belief is made in good faith. Section 7 goes on to explain that "[a] material representation is substantially correct if a prudent insurer would not consider the difference between what is represented and what is actually correct to be material."

The particular disclosure that is required is: every material circumstance which the insured knows or ought to know, or, failing that, disclosure which gives the insurer sufficient information to put a prudent insurer on notice that it needs to make further enquiries for the purpose of revealing those material circumstances. Before considering what that means, it can be noted that s 3(5) of the Insurance Act 2015 carves out what the insured needs to explain and disclose, such that in the absence of enquiry by the insurer there is no requirement on the insured to disclose a circumstance if: it diminishes the risk; the insurer knows it; the insurer ought to know it; the insurer is presumed to know it; or it is something as to which the insurer waives information.

The Insurance Act 2015 goes on to say what the insured and the insurer will be taken to know in s 5, with one provision presuming insurer knowledge of things which are common knowledge, and things which an insurer offering insurance of the class in question to insureds in the field of activity in question would reasonably be expected to know in the ordinary course of business.

As noted, s 3(4) of the Insurance Act 2015 asks for material circumstances to be disclosed, or at least sufficient details to allow an insurer to ask further questions, and section 7 offers some clarity as to what is meant by material. It provides that a circumstance or representation is material if it would influence the judgement of a prudent insurer in determining whether to take the risk and, if so, on what terms. It then offers examples of things which may be material circumstances, such as: special or unusual facts relating to the risk; any particular concerns which led the insured to seek insurance cover for the risk; and anything which those concerned with the class of insurance and field of activity in question would generally understand as being something that should be dealt with in a fair presentation of risks of the type in question.

To a large extent, older case law in this and other areas has now been superseded, but it may continue to have a legacy when it comes to consideration of matters not directly addressed in the 2015 Act. For example, when considering whether there was a breach of the duty of fair presentation in the case of *Young* v *Royal and Sun Alliance PLC* (2020), the insurer refused a claim on the basis of a failure to make a fair presentation of the risk, in particular because an individual did not disclose that he had been a director of four companies that had been dissolved after or placed into an insolvency process in the previous 5 years. The insured attempted to argue that any such breach had been waived by the insurer not following up in relation to a question about the director specifically going through such a process, but this was held not to be the case with reference to authorities from prior to the passing of the 2015 Act. The consequences that can follow from a breach are considered next.

Consequences of not meeting the disclosure duty As with the consumer disclosure duty, and along similar but slightly different lines, there is a statutory scheme to determine whether there are any consequences to a breach and, if so, what those consequences are. This non-consumer regime starts with the concept of the "qualifying breach" (in contrast to the "qualifying misrepresentation"), which again requires the insurer to demonstrate that, but for the breach, it would not have entered into the contract of insurance at all or would have done so only on different terms. Then, as with CIDRA, there are two levels of qualifying breach, being "deliberate or reckless" or neither deliberate nor reckless; the second category does not have a specific name. Where there is a deliberate or reckless qualifying breach, the consequences are severe for the insured: the insurer can avoid the contract, refuse all claims and (in contrast to the consumer regime) automatically keep any premiums already paid. For lesser breaches, the scheme is reminiscent to the consumer regime. A neither deliberate nor reckless breach that nevertheless induced the insurer to enter the contract allows the insurer to avoid the contract and reject all claims (but return the premiums). Alternatively, if the breach did not induce the formation of the contract but different terms from the insurer's norm were applied (other than amount of premium), the contract can be treated as if it had been entered into on those different terms, and, where the premium would have been higher, the cover provided is reduced proportionately to the lower premium actually paid. The formula that applies in relation to cover where there has been a lesser breach of the disclosure duty in both consumer and non-consumer situations uses the lesser "actual paid" figure divided by the greater "realistic price" that ought to have applied, through which you can work out how much cover was actually being paid for.

Duty not to make a fraudulent claim

An insurer is under no liability to indemnify an insured where a fraudulent claim is made, under s 12 of the Insurance Act 2015. This was the position at common law (see, for example, *Black King Shipping Corporation* v *Massie (The Litsion Pride)* (1985)) and the common law remains relevant in relation to determining what amounts to fraud, but s 12(1) of the Insurance Act 2015 now provides that where the insured makes a fraudulent claim the insurer is not liable to pay that claim, may recover any sums paid by the insurer to the insured in respect of the claim, and may by notice to the insured treat the contract as having been terminated with effect from the time of the fraudulent act. Where the contract is brought to an end, no further claims will be honoured and there is no need to return any premiums. According to the case of *Versloot Dredging BV* v *HDI Gerling Industrie Versicherung AG ("The DC Merwestone")* (2017) the insured will not be penalised for a certain amount of embellishments in a claim where those "collateral lies" do not substantively affect matters.

EVENT INSURED

On grounds of public policy, the insurer will be entitled to avoid liability where it can demonstrate that the insured deliberately caused the loss suffered: *Beresford* v *Royal Insurance Co Ltd* (1938). Difficulties arise where the event insured is partly caused by the actions of the insured. In the case of *Dhak* v *Insurance Co of North America (UK) Ltd* (1996), an insured under a life assurance policy began abusing alcohol to relieve the pain caused by a back injury sustained at work. Tragically, she died 6 months later as a result of asphyxiation through intoxication. The insurer resisted liability on the ground of an exclusion in the life insurance policy in respect of death caused by deliberate means. The court held that the insurer was under no liability to pay out the insurance proceeds where the insured had deliberately engaged in the act of intoxicating herself and had taken a calculated risk. Of course, matters would have been different had the death been caused by accidental means.

UNFAIR TERMS IN CONSUMER INSURANCE CONTRACTS

The Consumer Rights Act 2015 provides in s 62 that an unfair term is not binding on a consumer, and s 62(4) then offers a view on what is unfair (as explained above in the Sale of Goods chapter). Insurance contracts are not carved out of the coverage of this regime, but a difficulty in its application to an insurance consumer is that terms relating to the main subject-matter of the contract or the price that are prominent to the average customer and transparent (that is to say, in plain and intelligible language) will avoid an assessment for fairness (s 64 CRA). This means that clearly set out points that go to price and/or what the contract is about will not be tested for fairness. Where the premium paid has been affected, and a consumer has a cheap premium because of a limited scope of cover, that is not subject to assessment for the very reason that premiums have been cheaper. Whilst it does remain possible that a more ancillary term in a consumer insurance contract could be called into question on the basis of unfairness, it is difficult to envisage CRA having much of a direct application in this field.

REGULATION OF INSURANCE ACTIVITIES

Insurance activity is heavily regulated in the UK. The Prudential Regulation Authority takes an interest in matters such as the solvency of insurance providers, and the Financial Conduct Authority has a regulatory role in relation to the conduct of insurance business. It is an offence to offer insurance products without appropriate regulatory approval, and a document known as the Insurance Conduct of Business Sourcebook (ICOBS) contains wide-ranging provisions regarding matters such as distance-selling of insurance and mandatory cooling-off (cancellation) periods for customers. If an insurance company falls short in relation to ICOBS, that might be relevant to a court action or in a claim to the Financial Ombudsman Service. The Financial Ombudsman Service itself offers a free and accessible dispute resolution resource for consumers with insurance products and can make legally binding awards up to a certain figure, offering an alternative route to litigation.

Essential Facts

- An insurance contract protects an insured against the occurrence of a particular misfortune or particular risks.
- An insurance contract does not require to be reduced to writing in order to be legally valid in terms of Scots law: s 1(1) of the Requirements of Writing (Scotland) Act 1995.
- An insurance contract is a contract whereby for some consideration, usually but not necessarily for periodical payments called premiums, a person secures some benefit, usually but not necessarily the payment of a sum of money, upon the happening of some event, which event is adverse to the interests of that person and which involves an element of uncertainty as to (a) whether it will happen or not, or (b) the time at which it will happen.
- A party to an insurance contract must have insurable interest in the subject-matter of insurance. Otherwise, the insurance contract is void.
- In the case of life assurance, the policy will be void where a person takes out a life assurance policy over the life of another person in which they have no pecuniary or financial interest.
- In the context of indemnity insurance, the insured must have a legal or an equitable interest in the property insured.

- A warranty is a fundamental term of an insurance policy and, where a warranty is breached, the insurer is discharged from liability under the contract with effect from the date of the breach until the breach is remedied (if remediation is possible).

- A contract of insurance was traditionally viewed as a contract "*uberrimae fidei*", ie one "of the utmost good faith", but statute has reformed the law to set out the insured's duty to disclose relevant information to the insurer and rules relating to fraudulent claims on the policy.

- Different standards of pre-contract disclosure apply to consumers and non-consumers, with consumers having a reactive duty to take reasonable care not to make a misrepresentation (in terms of the Consumer Insurance (Disclosure and Representations) Act 2012) and non-consumers having a proactive duty to make a fair presentation of the risk (in terms of the Insurance Act 2015). The consequences for a breach of the disclosure duty depend on whether the insurer was induced into contracting as a result of that breach.

- Where the insured makes a fraudulent claim, the insurer need not pay the claim, can recover any funds already paid, and can bring the insurance contract to an end.

Essential Cases

Prudential Insurance Co v Inland Revenue Commissioners (1904): describes the four elements within the definition of the contract of insurance.

Dalby v India and London Life Assurance Co (1854): for the purposes of life assurance, the insured must possess an insurable interest in the life assured at the date the policy of insurance is effected.

Turnbull & Co v Scottish Provident Institution (1896): a firm had a direct financial interest, and thus an insurable interest, in the life of a local agent in Iceland.

Macaura v Northern Assurance Co Ltd (1925): a creditor, sole shareholder and director of a company did not have an insurable interest in respect of timber owned by the company and so the contract of insurance was invalid.

Carter v Boehm (1766) and **Stewart v Morison (1779)**: a contract of insurance is traditionally a contract *"uberrimae fidei"*.

Young v Royal and Sun Alliance (2020): the duty of fair presentation was not met when there was a failure by the insured to disclose that he had been a director of four companies that had been through an insolvency process in the previous 5 years and this was not waived by the insurer not following up in relation to a question about the director specifically going through such a process.

Beresford v Royal Insurance Co Ltd (1938): on grounds of public policy, the insurer will be entitled to avoid liability where it can be demonstrated that the insured deliberately caused the loss suffered.

5 RIGHTS IN SECURITY

When traders sell their goods or services to a purchaser, they may be paid money or money's worth on delivery or completion of performance. Alternatively, and much more commonly, the trader will supply on credit. However, with credit comes the risk that the trader ultimately may not be paid. For that reason, the trader may call for security from the buyer or some other third party as protection. Likewise, where a lender extends a loan or other credit facilities to a borrower, in order to secure the repayment of the loan or credit plus interest and other costs, the lender will often seek security from the borrower or a third party. The security obtained by the lender may be granted by the borrower or the third party over their corporeal or incorporeal assets or the third party may agree to repay the loan if the borrower fails to do so.

According to the classic description of "right in security" in Scots law, the term means "any right which a creditor may hold for ensuring the payment or satisfaction of his debt, distinct from, and in addition to, his right of action and execution against the debtor under the latter's personal obligation" (Gloag and Irvine, *Law of Rights in Security* (1897), pp 1–2). This additional right may take the form of a personal right in security or a real right in security.

PERSONAL RIGHTS IN SECURITY

Rights in security may be understood as personal or real rights and corresponding personal or real obligations. The difference between personal and real rights/obligations can be examined by first considering personal rights and obligations. Thus, where a trader or lender obtains a personal right to be paid the price from a third party for the goods sold or supplied or to have the loan repaid by a third party, that right translates into a corresponding obligation on the part of the third party to pay such price or repay such loan. Here, the obligation on the part of the third party is classified as a personal cautionary obligation or a personal guarantee and the trader or lender has a personal right to enforce that obligation against the third-party cautioner. Thus, where the trader or lender is unable to obtain payment of the price for the goods sold or supplied or the repayment of the loan from the purchaser or the borrower, the former may enforce its personal cautionary rights to call on the third party to pay the balance of the price or the balance of the sum or loan remaining unpaid. Those rights and the corresponding obligations on the part of the third party are not real since they do not involve the trader or lender having rights in relation to the property of the debtor or third party (and therefore priority in that party's insolvency). We will consider such personal cautionary obligations in detail in Chapter 6 on Cautionary Obligations.

REAL RIGHTS IN SECURITY

Personal cautionary obligations can be contrasted with real rights in security. Where a trader or lender obtains rights in the corporeal or incorporeal property of the purchaser or borrower in security for the payment of the price for the goods sold or supplied or the repayment of the loan, those rights are categorised as real rights. Thus, where the trader or lender is unable to obtain payment of the price for the goods sold or supplied or the repayment of the loan from the purchaser or the borrower, the former may enforce the real security which it has in the property of the latter in order to recover the balance of the price or the loan remaining unpaid. This is particularly valuable if the debtor is insolvent. We will examine such real rights in security in greater detail in this chapter.

THE ACCESSORY NATURE OF RIGHTS IN SECURITY

In both the cases of personal cautionary obligations and real rights in security, the personal rights and real rights are accessory and collateral in nature. That is to say that they are (a) accessory to the primary right of the trader to be paid by the purchaser for the price for the goods sold or supplied or for the lender to have the loan repaid from the borrower and (b) accessory to the corresponding primary obligation of the purchaser or the borrower to pay the trader the price for the goods sold or supplied or to repay the loan to the lender. Since these collateral rights are accessory or secondary in nature, they rely on the continuing existence of the primary right and corresponding primary obligation – when the primary right and obligation are extinguished, the general rule is that these accessory rights are also extinguished.

OUTLINE OF CHAPTER

In this chapter, we will explore *real rights in security* which may be sought and obtained by traders and lenders. The nature of the security depends on the underlying assets of the purchaser or borrower or third party which are covered by the security: for example, whether the assets are corporeal, incorporeal, heritable or moveable. In Chapter 6, we will subsequently move on to examine personal rights and obligations known as cautionary obligations. One of the legal considerations which distinguishes real rights in security from personal rights in security is that the latter do not require any publicity in order to be created, while some of the former do indeed entail some form of registration or other public act to make them legally effective.

FIXED SECURITIES AND FLOATING SECURITIES

Fixed security

A distinction can be made between fixed and floating rights in security. A fixed security constitutes a real right in favour of a creditor over an identified item (or items) of property. Since the property of the owner/debtor is the subject of a real right in security, the owner/debtor is disentitled from selling the assets free of that security without first obtaining the consent of the creditor or lender. To that extent, the owner's power of disposal over the secured assets is circumscribed.

Floating security

A floating security does not confer a real right in security in favour of the creditor or lender. Instead, the security hovers over the assets and undertaking of the granter. It is only on the occurrence of specific events that the law provides that the floating security converts into a fixed security, at least for certain purposes. Scots law recognises many forms of fixed security which are available over different kinds of property, whereas the recognition of floating security is far more limited, with the floating charge being the principal and undisputed example.

VOLUNTARY SECURITIES AND SECURITIES ARISING BY OPERATION OF LAW

Voluntary security

A real right in security can be created voluntarily by a debtor in favour of a creditor. Conversely, the security can arise automatically by operation of law. This means that securities arising by operation of law emerge without the agreement of the parties, that is, involuntarily. The form of the voluntary real right in security is conditioned by the nature of the security property. For example, whether the property is: (a) corporeal or incorporeal; and (b) heritable or moveable in nature dictates the form of the security.

Securities arising by operation of law

The nature of the security which emerges by operation of law is dependent on the form of property to which it relates. The two principal securities which arise by operation of law are lien (which may be special or general) and hypothec (for example, landlord's hypothec). These securities are available to a creditor where the debtor has failed to make payment of a sum of money due to the creditor and the property is in possession of the debtor (in the case of lien) or the debtor's moveables are on commercial rented premises (in the case of landlord's hypothec, which has been restricted by s 208(3) of the Bankruptcy and Diligence etc (Scotland) Act 2007 to only apply in a commercial context). In this chapter, we will analyse voluntary securities. Due to space constraints, we will not be examining securities arising by operation of law and on these you should refer to a specialist Scots property or commercial law text.

VOLUNTARY SECURITIES: RIGHTS IN SECURITY OVER CORPOREAL MOVEABLES

Introduction

Rights in security over corporeal moveables, that is to say items that have a physical presence but are not, or are not connected to, land, may be divided into possessory securities and non-possessory securities. While a possessory security involves the owner/debtor relinquishing possession of its corporeal moveable assets to the creditor, a non-possessory security involves no transfer of possession from the owner/debtor to the creditor. Scots law has traditionally been hostile to the constitution of non-possessory rights in security. This hostility was and is based on the principle of Scots property law which requires some form of publicity in connection with the creation or transfer of real rights. Since the constitution of rights in security over corporeal moveable assets involves the creation of real rights, such publicity is demanded by the law and delivery from the debtor to the lender is the traditional form of publicity required. However, a number of limited categories of non-possessory securities have been recognised by Scots law. The reason for the introduction of these limited forms of non-possessory security is tied up with the obvious impracticability of a debtor transferring possession of its moveable assets to creditors or lenders in the modern commercial climate. For example, a lender will not be particularly keen for its debtor customers to deliver their moveable assets (such as cranes, combine harvesters and other plant and machinery) to its offices. Moreover, the owner/debtor does not wish to be deprived of those moveable assets which it requires to carry on its ordinary day-to-day business. For that reason, Scots law now supports the constitution of some non-possessory forms of real rights in security over moveable assets as a means of recognising commercial reality.

Possessory securities: pledge

Introduction

Pledge is the main form of possessory security over corporeal moveables. The owner/debtor undertakes to pay the creditor or lender a sum of money and in security of that obligation duly grants a pledge which involves the transfer of possession of certain identified moveable assets of the owner/debtor to the creditor or lender. If the owner/debtor fails to repay the sums owed, the creditor or lender will normally be able to sell the property pledged to recover the balance of the sums owed.

Delivery

In *Pattison's Trustee* v *Liston* (1893), Lord Trayner stated that in order to validly constitute a pledge, delivery of the property which is the subject of the pledge is necessary. The case of *Bank of Scotland* v *Hutchison, Main & Co Ltd Liquidators* (1914) decided that an obligation on the owner/debtor to deliver the assets or property to the creditor or the lender is insufficient to create a pledge. Such an obligation merely confers a personal right in favour of the creditor or lender which does not defeat the claims of a trustee in sequestration or liquidator appointed over the estate of the owner/debtor. It is only where the real right in security of pledge has been constituted by delivery that the rights of competing claimants to the assets of the debtor (such as a trustee in sequestration or liquidator appointed over the estate of the owner/debtor) will be defeated. Moreover, a sham sale entered into between the owner/debtor and creditor or lender (in terms of which the owner/debtor purports to "sell" their moveable assets to the creditor while holding on to possession and use of those assets in return for "payment" of a sum of money) is treated by Scots law as invalid as a right in security by virtue of *Allan* v *Galbraith* (1902) and does not constitute a valid sale (by virtue of s 62(4) of the Sale of Goods Act 1979 and the delivery requirement at common law).

Forms of delivery

While it is pivotal that delivery is required to constitute the pledge, it is not always the case that physical delivery is necessary, despite some authority to that effect (eg *Hamilton* v *Western Bank* (1856)). Delivery may be actual, symbolic or constructive. Actual delivery is straightforward to understand. Meanwhile, symbolic delivery entails the transfer of the documents of title to the assets to the creditor or lender: see, for example, *Hayman* v *McLintock* (1907) where the owner/debtor delivered bills of lading in relation to certain goods to various creditors and lenders. Constructive delivery involves the intermediation of an independent third-party keeper of assets owned by the owner/debtor. One example is where an independent third party keeping goods on behalf of the owner/debtor, for example a storekeeper, is given instructions by the owner/debtor to hold those assets or goods on behalf of the creditor or lender. The keeper must receive intimation of instructions from the owner/debtor. Otherwise, the case of *Inglis* v *Robertson & Baxter* (1898) stipulates that an effective pledge will not have been created.

Possessory securities: pawn

A particular type of pledge is pawn under ss 8(1) and 189(1) of the Consumer Credit Act 1974. Any pledge given by an individual in return for the provision of credit will constitute a pawn. Section 114(1) of the Consumer Credit Act 1974 stipulates that the creditor is under an obligation to give the owner/debtor a receipt in the prescribed form in exchange for the delivery of the items pawned. In terms of ss 116 and 120(1)(b) of the Consumer Credit Act 1974, any item pawned is redeemable at any time within 6 months after it was taken, or such other longer period as the parties may agree. If the owner/debtor fails to redeem within this prescribed period, by virtue of the terms of s 116(3) of the Consumer Credit Act 1974, the owner/debtor continues to enjoy the right to redeem until the creditor sells the articles and realises the pawn. However, there is an exception which applies where the credit extended to the owner/debtor is £75 or less and the period of 6 months has expired. Here, s 120(1)(a) of the Consumer Credit Act 1974 directs that property in the items pawned passes automatically to the creditor at the end of that period. Section 117(1) of the Consumer Credit Act 1974 states that on the owner/debtor surrendering the pawn receipt and paying the amount owing, the creditor must redeliver the items pawned to the owner/debtor and the pawn is considered to have been redeemed. Where the owner/debtor has misplaced or lost the pawn receipt, they may tender a statutory declaration in the prescribed form or a written statement (where the creditor agrees and the credit does not exceed £75) in accordance with s 118 of the Consumer Credit Act 1974. Section 121 of the Consumer Credit Act 1974 deals with the powers of the creditor to sell the articles pawned where the redemption period of 6 months or longer has expired. Here, it is stipulated that the creditor may sell the pawned articles after giving the owner/debtor not less than the prescribed period of notice of their intention to sell, indicating in the notice the asking price. Subsequent to the sale, the creditor must give the owner/debtor prescribed information in writing as to the sale, its proceeds and expenses. Where there is a surplus in the proceeds of sale vis-à-vis the sum owing, then the debt secured by the pawn is discharged and any surplus must be paid by the creditor to the owner/debtor.

Non-possessory securities

Scots common law was traditionally unsympathetic to the recognition of non-possessory forms of security over the corporeal moveable assets of a debtor. Over time, however, certain types were received into the law of Scotland. For example, for obvious reasons, it was recognised that it was impracticable for ships, sea-bearing vessels and cargo to be pledged, since it was plain that it would be more or less impossible to arrange for delivery of these moveables to the creditor. For that reason, Bell's *Principles*, ss 452–456 states that Scots common law recognised the bond of bottomry, which is a right in security granted over ships, and the bond of respondentia, which could be granted as security over a ship's cargo. The position with regard to ships is now governed by s 16 of the Merchant Shipping Act 1995, which provides for a statutory form of mortgage over a ship or a share in a ship without delivery or the transfer of possession to the creditor. Paragraph 7 of Sch 1 to the Merchant Shipping Act 1995 directs that the mortgage must be registered in the British Register of Shipping to be valid. It is equally possible to create statutory mortgages over registered aircraft in terms of s 86 of the Civil Aviation Act 1982 and the Mortgaging of Aircraft Order 1972 (SI 1972/1268).

The floating charge was introduced into Scots law by legislation in 1961 and is a key form of non-possessory security over corporeal moveables and all other types of property. It is discussed in more detail below. In addition, it should be noted that it is possible to use the reservation or transfer of ownership to create functional securities over corporeal moveables: that is, rather than obtaining a subordinate real right in security in the property of the debtor, the creditor retains or obtains ownership for security purposes. Reservation of title arrangements and certain sale and leaseback transactions, especially those with an option to repurchase, are principal examples, albeit that the latter may require some form of delivery to the creditor initially to transfer ownership before possession is given back to the debtor.

VOLUNTARY SECURITIES: RIGHTS IN SECURITY OVER INCORPOREAL MOVEABLES

Introduction

A debtor may create security over their incorporeal moveables: for example, shares, patents, copyright, trade marks, debts and other accounts receivable, etc. Some incorporeal moveables are incapable of being security property, such as alimentary rights and rights involving *delectus personae*.

Constitution

A fixed security over incorporeal moveables is effected by the debtor transferring title to the creditor or lender under a document referred to as an assignation. Thus, title is actually assigned (transferred) from the debtor to the creditor or lender. The first stage of the assignation of the specified incorporeal moveable property is effective to confer a personal right in favour of the creditor or lender. The second stage entails intimation of the assignation to the account debtor in the relevant obligation and it is this second stage that functions to confer a real right in the asset in favour of the creditor/lender. The account debtor in the case of an insurance policy will be the insurance company, whereas, in the case of debts and accounts receivable owed to the debtor, it will be the third-party debtor who is due to pay such sums to the debtor. In technical terms, since no subordinate real right in security is created in the debtor's property and instead the transfer of title/ownership is being used for security purposes, assignation in security is a functional security.

Intimation

Without intimation, which may be considered the equivalent of delivery (in the case of corporeal moveables), no security will be created in favour of the creditor or lender as assignee. Thus, intimation is required to complete the right of the creditor or lender as assignee. If the creditor or lender has had an incorporeal moveable assigned to them without intimation, then all they have is a personal right to receive the incorporeal moveable asset and their interests are susceptible to defeat by other interested third parties: for example, liquidators, trustees in sequestration, etc. For that reason, intimation, which transfers the incorporeal property and thus creates the security, is critically important. The Transmission of Moveable Property (Scotland) Act 1862 provides for forms of assignation and intimation. However, it is not an absolute requirement that these forms be followed. There is also no particular requirement as to the words required for an assignation or intimation, and different forms of intimation are possible, but there must be a clearly expressed intention to assign (*Carter* v *McIntosh* (1862)). In terms of intimation, the principal question is whether the facts and circumstances of the particular case demonstrate that intimation has been made. Furthermore, while intimation to the third-party account debtor may be made in writing, the legal equivalent of a formal intimation will be implied by the law in certain circumstances: for example, where it is unrealistic to suggest that the third-party account debtor is unaware of the fact of the assignation. Examples include effecting diligence (Erskine, *Institute*, III, 5, 4) over the assets of the third-party account debtor or the raising of court action against them (*Whyte* v *Neish* (1622)). Once the intimation has been sent, there is no requirement that the third-party account debtor must acknowledge it for valid intimation to have been made (*Christie Owen & Davies plc t/a Christie & Co* v *Campbell* (2009)), albeit that this may be useful for evidential purposes. Moreover, the third-party account debtor may be personally barred from arguing that intimation has not been effected where he has previously promised to make payment to the assignee (*Home and Elphinstone* v *Murray* (1674)). Since it is critical to intimate to a third-party account debtor the existence of the assignation in order to create the security, it follows that it is not possible (or at least highly impracticable) to effect a security over property that does not exist or that is not owned by the owner/debtor at the point in time at which the attempt was made to effect the intimation.

Impossibility of intimation

On occasion, intimation will be impossible. Where the incorporeal moveables in question are patents, copyright or trade marks, there will be no account debtor to whom intimation may be made, since these rights do not involve corresponding obligations or duties on the part of third-party account debtors to make payment or otherwise, so alternative publicity must be sought. In the case of patents or trade marks, ss 31– 33 of the Patents Act 1977 and ss 22–24 of the Trade Marks Act 1994 stipulate that registration is required in order to create the security. For copyright, there is no register of copyrights and thus an assignation without intimation or registration is sufficient to confer a security in favour of a creditor or lender (s 90 of the Copyright, Designs and Patents Act 1988). In the case of shares, registration in the company's register of members is required to establish the security over the shares in favour of the creditor or lender (*Guild* v *Young* (1884)), and this is an outright transfer (*Farstad Supply A/S* v *Enviroco* (2011)).

Assignatus utitur jure auctoris

Once the security over the incorporeal moveable property has been constituted in favour of the creditor or lender, the principle of *assignatus utitur jure auctoris* applies to condition the extent of the creditor or lender's rights. This principle holds that the assignee (ie the creditor or lender) obtains no better right than the cedent/assignor (ie the debtor). Thus, if the account debtor has a defence to the claim of the cedent/assignor, that defence is also available to the account debtor against the claim of the assignee (ie the creditor or lender). One can conceptualise the principle of *assignatus utitur jure auctoris* as being concerned with the enforcement of the security by the creditor or lender. The case of *Shiells* v *Ferguson, Davidson & Co* (1876) provides a good example of the rule in operation. Here, the debt assigned in security from the debtor to the creditor had been extinguished by virtue of the operation of compensation (a form of set-off of money claims) prior to the perfection of the assignation in security. Since this had occurred, the creditor's security was worthless and could not be enforced against the account debtor.

VOLUNTARY SECURITIES: RIGHTS IN SECURITY OVER HERITABLE PROPERTY

Introduction

A debtor may create a real right in security over their heritable property, such as land or buildings. Where a creditor takes a standard security, they are referred to as the "heritable creditor". Section 9(3) of the Conveyancing and Feudal Reform (Scotland) Act 1970 (the "1970 Act") directs that the standard security is the only competent heritable security which can be granted in security over land or a real right in land to a creditor or lender for the purpose of securing a debt. In terms of s 9(8)(c) of the 1970 Act, the definition of "debt" is wide enough to encompass obligations to repay fixed and fluctuating sums of money, non-monetary obligations *ad factum praestandum* (which enjoin a person to undertake a particular task) and annuities. However, rent and other periodical sums payable in respect of land are expressly excluded. The standard security over any land or real right in land is to be registered in the Land Register and the meaning of a "real right in land" is set out in s 9(8)(b) of the 1970 Act. Once registered in the Land Register, a standard security will confer a real right in security in favour of the creditor in terms of s 11(1) of the 1970 Act.

Form of standard security

Section 9(2) of the 1970 Act directs that the standard security must conform with one of the prescribed forms set out in Sch 2 to the 1970 Act. Form A ought to be used where the personal obligation to repay the debt is included in the standard security instrument and Form B where the personal obligation is constituted in a separate instrument.

Standard conditions

The 1970 Act contains standard conditions which govern the relationship between the debtor and the heritable creditor and the powers and rights of the latter. Section 11(2) of the 1970 Act provides that the standard conditions outlined in Sch 3 to the 1970 Act are incorporated into every standard security, unless varied in accordance with the provisions of s 11(3) of the 1970 Act. Section 11(3) directs that some of the standard conditions may not be varied, namely the conditions relating to redemption, powers of sale and foreclosure. The standard conditions delimited in Sch 3 comprise 12 separate conditions. Condition 1 imposes obligations of maintenance and repair on the debtor, while Condition 2 stipulates that the debtor is obliged to complete any unfinished buildings to the satisfaction of the creditor. The other conditions impose obligations on the debtor to perform all monetary and non-monetary obligations in respect of the land: for example, to pay rates and other land taxes, to insure the buildings, to comply with planning obligations and to refrain from letting the subjects secured without the creditor's prior written consent. The latter condition is particularly important, since the case of *Trade Development Bank v Warriner and Mason (Scotland) Ltd* (1980) demonstrates that a tenant's lease of the security property can be reduced by the creditor, unless the creditor had knowledge that the tenant had a real right of lease at the time when the security was granted. Condition 7 provides the creditor with the power to perform obligations which the debtor has failed to perform in terms of the standard conditions and to charge the debtor for the costs of performance of such obligations. Condition 8 empowers the creditor to "call up" the standard security in accordance with the provisions of s 19 of the 1970 Act, that is, to take action to enforce the standard security in order to recoup the indebtedness of the debtor to the creditor. Condition 9 states that a debtor is held to be in default of their obligations when a calling-up notice has been served but not complied with, when they have failed to comply with any other requirement of the standard security or when the proprietor of the security property (usually the debtor) has become insolvent. Condition 10 regulates the rights of the creditor on the debtor's default and Condition 11 sets out the rules with regard to the debtor's entitlement to exercise their right to redeem the standard security. Finally, Condition 12 specifies that the debtor is liable for the costs of preparing and registering the standard security.

Ranking

Standard securities generally rank in accordance with their registration dates. However, in terms of *Scotlife Homes (No 2) Ltd* v *Muir* (1994), it is open to the parties to regulate the order of priority by agreement. A ranking agreement may be registered in the Land Register (s 13(4)). Furthermore, section 13(1) of the 1970 Act stipulates that where a first-ranking standard security holder receives notice of the creation of a subsequent ranking standard security, the first-ranking standard security is restricted to (a) the original debt incurred, (b) any further advances which the creditor is under a contractual obligation to make, (c) interest chargeable on such advances, and (d) any expenses or outlays reasonably incurred in the exercise of any power conferred by the security.

Competitions

Where a creditor holds some other security from the debtor, for example a creditor who has undertaken diligence, the holder of the standard security will find itself engaged in a competition. In the event that the debtor has been inhibited prior to the debtor granting the standard security to the creditor, the inhibition will defeat the right of the creditor in the standard security (*Baird and Brown* v *Stirrat's Tr* (1872)). However, where the inhibition is effected after the grant of a standard security, the standard security will take precedence over the inhibition (*Campbell's Trs* v *De Lisle's Exrs* (1870)). For further details about inhibition and other diligences, see Chapter 10 on Diligence.

When the debtor enters into sequestration, liquidation, receivership or administration, the rights of the secured creditor in terms of the standard security will be preserved. Thus, since the standard security is a fixed security, the trustee in sequestration, liquidator, receiver or administrator will be required to obtain the consent of the holder of the standard security prior to sale of the secured property or seek the authority of the court to sell. Moreover, the secured creditor will be paid out in priority to lower-ranking secured creditors and unsecured creditors on the distribution of the estate by the trustee in sequestration, liquidator, receiver or administrator to the creditors.

Discharge

The relevant rules governing discharge are contained in s 17 of the 1970 Act. The security property may be disburdened from the standard security by the registration of a discharge in terms of the prescribed form in Sch 4 to the 1970 Act. Of course, the creditor is only likely to consent to, and execute, such a discharge if it is satisfied that the outstanding indebtedness owed by the debtor has been repaid in full. Subject to agreement to the contrary, s 18 of the 1970 Act and Standard Condition 11 regulate the redemption of standard securities. Here, it is directed that the debtor is entitled to redeem the security on giving 2 months' notice of their intention to do so and in accordance with the prescribed forms set out in Sch 5 to the Act. The redemption notice may be given by the debtor, or their successors in title, assignees or representatives to the creditor, or their successors in title, assignees or representatives. It is also possible for the heritable creditor to restrict their security, that is to disburden a portion of the land while retaining security over the remainder, by deed of restriction.

Enforcement

Prior to 2010, it appeared that a heritable creditor had a number of options to enforce the standard security, including a default notice upon the debtor in conformity with Form B of Sch 6 to the 1970 Act in terms of s 21 of the 1970 Act and Standard Condition 9 and a calling-up notice upon the proprietor of the subjects encumbered by the standard security (usually the debtor) in conformity with Form A of Sch 6 to the 1970 Act under s 19 of the 1970 Act. A third option was obtaining a warrant from the court in terms of s 24 of the 1970 Act. It is, however, no longer possible to use the notice of default route for monetary obligations, including the debt to be paid, so the remainder of this chapter will only look at calling-up notices and the s 24 warrant.

Calling-up notice

The service of a calling-up notice allows the power of sale available under the 1970 Act to be exercised.

Prior to 2010, it was thought that the calling-up notice was a possible step on the route to enforcing the standard security, but the important case of *Royal Bank of Scotland plc* v *Wilson* (2010) held that it was actually a *necessary* step. The relevant provision of the 1970 Act (s 19(1)) uses the word "shall", and in *Royal Bank of Scotland plc* v *Wilson* the Supreme Court held (contrary to prevailing practice) that this word should be interpreted so as to make a calling-up notice a mandatory step before exercising any power of sale.

The calling-up notice must give the debtor a period of at least 2 months to pay. Where the debtor fails to comply with the calling-up notice, the creditor is entitled to exercise the statutory default powers which are set out in Standard Condition 10(2)–(7) (found in Sch 3 to the 1970 Act), namely the power of sale, the power to enter into possession of the secured subjects and receive or recover the rents of those subjects, the power to let the secured subjects or any part thereof, the power to carry out necessary repairs and the power to apply to the court for a decree of foreclosure. This is subject to an important control in relation to residential properties, considered below.

Powers under Standard Condition 10(2)–(7)

When exercising the power of sale, the creditor must take into account the interests of the debtor. Therefore, where the proceeds of the sale of the security subjects exceed the level of the outstanding indebtedness, the creditor must account to the debtor for the surplus. Section 25 of the 1970 Act stipulates that the creditor may sell by private bargain or public roup (ie auction) and the creditor is under a duty to advertise the sale and to take all reasonable steps to ensure that the price at which the subjects or any part are sold is the best that can reasonably be obtained. The creditor may be liable in damages to the debtor where it breaches its duties under s 25 of the 1970 Act (*Royal Bank of Scotland* v *A and M Johnston* (1987) and *Bank of Credit* v *Thomson* (1987)). However, it is evidentially very difficult for a debtor to satisfy the court that the creditor has breached such duties (*Dick* v *Clydesdale Bank plc* (1991)). Once the security property has been sold by the creditor, the proceeds of sale must be distributed in accordance with s 27 of the 1970 Act, namely: first, the expenses of the sale must be paid; second, sums which are due under any prior security to which the sale was not made subject; third, any sums due under the standard security and other securities of equal ranking; and, finally, sums due under securities which are postponed to the standard security in accordance with their ranking. Any remaining residue is to be given to the party entitled to the security subjects.

The creditor also has a default power to recover any rents due from tenants of the security property from the date the creditor enters possession, but not arrears of rent (*UCB Bank Ltd* v *Hire Foulis (In Liquidation)* (1999)). The other default power of the creditor which is extremely important is the right of foreclosure, that is, Standard Condition 10(7). The foreclosure right enables the creditor to take ownership of the security property. Section 28 of the 1970 Act stipulates conditions for the exercise of the right of foreclosure. Section 28(5)–(6) of the 1970 Act state that the effect of the registration of a decree of foreclosure is that the creditor is vested in the subjects, the debtor's right to redeem the standard security is extinguished, the subjects are disburdened of any standard security and all other postponed securities and diligences and the creditor is given the same right as the debtor to redeem any security ranking prior to, or equally with, their own security.

Residential subjects

The Home Owner and Debtor Protection (Scotland) Act 2010 amends the 1970 Act by requiring the creditor to appear before the sheriff to obtain a s 24 warrant when seeking to enforce in relation to land used to any extent for residential purposes (s 24(1B)). A heritable creditor is not able to obtain such a warrant without first complying with the pre-action requirements contained in s 24A, including clear information about the terms of the standard security, the amount due to the creditor under the standard security (including any arrears and any charges in respect of late payment or redemption) and any other obligation under the standard security in respect of which the debtor is in default. Further requirements are laid down in the Applications by Creditors (Pre-Action Requirements) (Scotland) Order 2010 (SSI 2010/317).

The court may not grant an application unless it is satisfied that the creditor has complied with all the above requirements and that it is reasonable in the circumstances of the case to do so. In making its decision, the court is to have regard to the matters set out in s 24(7), including:

- the nature of and reasons for the default;
- the ability of the debtor to fulfil within a reasonable time the obligations under the standard security in respect of which the debtor is in default;
- any action taken by the creditor to assist the debtor to fulfil those obligations;
- where appropriate, participation by the debtor in a debt payment programme approved under Pt 1 of the Debt Arrangement and Attachment (Scotland) Act 2002; and
- the ability of the debtor and any other person residing at the security subjects to secure reasonable alternative accommodation.

There is also provision for entitled residents to involve themselves in the court proceedings (ss 24B–24D). When all of these statutory steps are coupled with the necessity of a calling-up notice to unlock certain enforcement powers of the creditor, it can be seen that a creditor must exercise great care to comply with these steps and therefore be in a position that the court will grant an order to exercise any of the remedies which the creditor is entitled to exercise on the debtor's default.

VOLUNTARY SECURITIES: FLOATING CHARGE

Introduction

The floating charge is an important form of non-possessory security in Scots law. Section 462 of the Companies Act 1985 enables a company to grant a floating charge as security for a debt or other obligation. Certain other types of incorporated entity, such as limited liability partnerships, co-operative societies, community benefit societies and building societies are also able to create floating charges but individuals and ordinary partnerships are not able to do so. When it is created, a floating charge hovers over all (or part) of the property and undertaking of the granter, as that property changes from time to time. A key advantage of a floating charge is that it can encompass all types of property: corporeal and incorporeal, heritable and moveable, and can even be used for new forms of property such as digital assets. In addition, a floating charge covers present and future property of the granter (once the granter acquires the property). However, the floating charge does not confer a real right in security over any particular asset. Thus, the granter of the floating charge may sell and buy assets without obtaining the prior consent of the floating charge holder in relation to such dealings. Only when it attaches upon certain events taking place does a floating charge take on characteristics of a fixed security and thereby stops the granter dealing with the property without the charge holder's consent (see further below).

Constitution

Unlike other security rights, a floating charge does not require an act of publicity for its creation. The execution of a floating charge document (instrument) and the giving of it to the grantee (which is a private act) will create the security. However, it is necessary for the floating charge documentation to be registered in the Companies Register within 21 days after the date of its creation (ss 859A–859E of the Companies Act 2006). If the registration requirements are not complied with, s 859H of the Companies Act 2006 provides that the charge is void against a liquidator, administrator or creditor of the granter company. These registration requirements also apply to other forms of voluntary security created by companies, including standard securities and assignations in security (but not pledges).

Attachment ("crystallisation") and enforcement

A floating charge attaches (sometimes also referred to as "crystallisation") upon certain events taking place. At this point it ceases to hover and instead attaches to all of the property and undertaking of the granter stipulated to be covered by the security in terms of the floating charge instrument (in practice, it is standard for the floating charge instrument to state that all of the assets and undertaking of the granter are subject to the floating charge). It should be noted, however, that not all property owned by the granter will be attached by the floating charge. In *Sharp* v *Thomson* (1997) a floating charge was granted by a company and some years later the company sold a flat, with consideration paid, entry into the property was taken by the purchasers and a disposition was delivered to them. Yet before recording of the disposition, the floating charge attached. Despite ownership not having transferred to the purchasers, the House of Lords held that the floating charge did not attach to the property and the purchasers obtained the property unencumbered by the security. While the precise ratio of the case is still not certain, at least some property may leave the "property and undertaking" of a selling company for floating charge purposes at an earlier stage than is the case for the transfer of property under general property law.

The effect of crystallisation is that the charge is treated as if it were a fixed security over the property of the granter (for a number of purposes) and those assets are available to a liquidator, receiver or administrator to ingather and sell in order to make good the sums owing to creditors. The charge crystallises on the appointment of a liquidator (in terms of s 463(1) of the Companies Act 1985), the appointment of a receiver (in terms of s 53(7) or 54(6) of the Insolvency Act 1986), a court consenting to a distribution by an administrator to a party other than a secured creditor or preferential creditor (para 115(1A)–(1B) of Sch B1 to the Insolvency Act 1986), or on an administrator filing a notice to the effect that they think the company has insufficient property to enable a distribution to be made to the company's unsecured creditors (para 115(2)–(3) of Sch B1 to the Insolvency Act 1986).

Ranking

Real security rights ordinarily rank according to their date of creation, *prior tempore potior jure*. A fixed security is created on the date that it is constituted as a real right. In the case of a pledge, the date of creation will be the date of delivery and the date of creation of a standard security is the date on which the standard security is registered in the Land Register. The ranking rules for floating charges are, however, rather complicated and are outlined in s 464 of the Companies Act 1985. The default position is that a floating charge ranks from the date of its attachment against other voluntary security rights, including standard securities and pledges. In a competition between floating charges, the date of registration in the Companies Register is the relevant factor. In the vast majority of cases, however, a floating charge instrument will have a "negative pledge" prohibiting or restricting the creation of subsequent voluntary securities (fixed and floating) with priority over the floating charge. The effect of this is that any such securities granted after the creation of the floating charge will rank behind it (s 464(1)(a) and (1A) of the Companies Act 1985). It is also possible for floating charge holders and fixed security holders to change the priority of ranking within a floating charge or standard security instrument, provided that the agreement of all security holders affected is obtained (s 464(1)(b) of the Companies Act 1985).

It should be noted that a negative pledge will not affect involuntary security, including fixed securities arising by operation of law and diligences. A fixed security arising by operation of law always has priority over a floating charge (s 464(2) of the Companies Act 1985). A floating charge is also subject to the rights of any person who has effectually executed diligence on the property prior to the attachment of the floating charge (s 463(1)(a) of the Companies Act 1985, s 60(1) of the Insolvency Act 1986, and *MacMillan* v *T Leith Developments Ltd* (2017); see also Chapter 10 below).

FUTURE REFORM

The Scottish Law Commission (SLC) has proposed reforms to the law of security rights (see *Report on Moveable Transactions* (2017)). The SLC recommends the introduction of a new form of non-possessory security, a statutory pledge, which would be created by registration in a new Register of Statutory Pledges and which could cover present and future property. The security would be available for corporeal moveables and certain types of incorporeal moveable property, including intellectual property. In addition, the SLC recommends reforms to the law of assignation, including the introduction of registration in a Register of Assignations as an alternative to intimation, amendments to intimation requirements, and improvements to the law of possessory pledges, such as legislative confirmation that actual delivery is not required to create the security. At the time of writing, the Moveable Transactions (Scotland) Bill, which would implement various recommendations of the SLC, is progressing through the Scottish Parliament.

The SLC is now working on a project examining the reform of the law of heritable securities. This includes consideration of pre-default issues and default and enforcement matters for standard securities. The project may also lead to significant reform in the years ahead.

Essential Facts

- Rights in security may confer personal or real rights in favour of a creditor.
- Real rights in security confer rights in security in favour of a creditor over the property of another party.
- Rights in security are accessory to the primary right of the trader or lender to be paid or to have the loan repaid.
- Real rights in security may be fixed or floating.
- Real rights in security may be voluntary or arise by operation of law.
- Pledge is a real right in security which a creditor may take over the corporeal assets of a debtor or third party, and in a consumer context "pawn" is the term used for the security.
- Rights in security are ordinarily constituted over incorporeal moveables by assignation and intimation or registration.
- Intimation will be effective where the facts and circumstances of the particular case demonstrate that intimation has been made to the third-party account debtor.
- A standard security is the only form of voluntary heritable security available over land and real rights in land.
- The Conveyancing and Feudal Reform (Scotland) Act 1970 regulates the constitution, ranking, discharge and enforcement of standard securities.
- A floating charge is a form of non-possessory right in security which is not fixed over any of the assets of the debtor. It becomes fixed (for certain purposes) only on the occurrence of attachment (crystallisation).

Essential Cases

Pattison's Tr v Liston (1893): in order to validly constitute a pledge, delivery of the property which is the subject of the pledge is necessary.

Bank of Scotland v Hutchison, Main & Co Ltd Liquidators (1914): an obligation on the owner/debtor to deliver the assets or property to the creditor or the lender is insufficient to create a pledge.

Hayman v McLintock (1907): symbolic delivery entails the transfer of the documents of title to the assets to the creditor or lender.

Inglis v Robertson & Baxter (1898): where a storekeeper is not given instructions by the owner/debtor to hold particular assets or goods on behalf of the creditor or lender, constructive delivery will not have taken place in order to validly create a pledge.

Carter v McIntosh (1862): there is no particular form of words required for an assignation but there must be a clearly expressed intention to assign.

Christie Owen & Davies plc t/a Christie & Co v Campbell (2009): once a letter of intimation has been sent, there is no requirement that the third-party account debtor must acknowledge it for valid intimation to have been made.

Home and Elphinstone v Murray (1674): a third-party account debtor may be personally barred from arguing that intimation has not been effected where they have previously promised to make payment to the assignee.

Shiells v Ferguson, Davidson & Co (1876): an example of *assignatus utitur jure auctoris* in operation.

Trade Development Bank v Warriner and Mason (Scotland) Ltd (1980): a tenant's lease of the security property can be reduced by the creditor, unless the creditor had knowledge that the tenant had a real right of lease at the time when the security was granted.

Baird and Brown v Stirrat's Tr (1872): in a competition between an inhibitor and a heritable creditor, the standard security will not cut down the inhibition where the former was effected prior to the constitution of the latter.

Campbell's Trs v De Lisle's Exrs (1870): where an inhibition is effected after the grant of a standard security, the standard security will take precedence over the inhibition.

Royal Bank of Scotland plc v Wilson (2010): a calling-up notice is necessary in all cases where the creditor requires discharge of the debt secured and, failing discharge, where the creditor wishes to exercise the power of sale.

Sharp v Thomson (1997): a floating charge does not attach to property that is no longer in the granter company's "property and undertaking" and heritable property was held to leave the granter's property and undertaking prior to the registration of a disposition in favour of the purchasers, which is necessary to transfer ownership under general property law.

6 CAUTIONARY OBLIGATIONS

At the beginning of Chapter 5 on Rights in Security, consideration was given to the distinction between personal and real rights which function to provide security to a creditor or lender. That chapter moved on to examine real rights in security. In this chapter, we will explore personal rights and obligations in more detail. The adjective attached to these rights and obligations underscores that they are personal. That is to say that they are not enforceable over an identified item of property. Instead, the obligation to make good the debt owed to the creditor is imposed on a legal person such as an individual, partnership or company. The law refers to that third party as a cautioner and the obligations imposed on that cautioner are referred to as cautionary obligations. In a layperson's terms, the cautionary obligation is a guarantee and the cautioner is a guarantor.

PARTIES

The law of caution involves three parties. First, there is the principal debtor who has a personal obligation to pay sums to the second party, namely the creditor. There will usually be a contract between the principal debtor and the creditor recognising this personal obligation. However, such a contract is not essential. The arrangement usually entails a separate contract between the creditor and the cautioner known as a contract of cautionry. Such contract provides that the cautioner will pay a certain sum of money (usually the principal debt, plus interest on that sum and the creditor's costs and expenses) or perform a particular obligation in the event that the principal debtor fails to pay such sum or perform such obligation. This obligation which burdens the cautioner is referred to as the cautionary obligation. The cautionary obligation is accessory in nature in the sense that it rests on the principal obligation of the principal debtor. There is a common-law rule that the cautionary obligation is not an independent obligation and, generally, for the cautionary obligation to exist there must be a principal obligation. However, there is an exception whereby the principal obligation need not exist when the cautionary obligation is entered into, so long as it is contemplated in the future.

CONSTITUTION AND FORM OF CAUTIONARY OBLIGATIONS

Writing

Generally, cautionary obligations do not require to be committed to writing in order to be validly constituted, but there are important exceptions to that rule. Section 1(2)(a)(ii) of the Requirements of Writing (Scotland) Act 1995 stipulates that writing is required for the proper constitution of a gratuitous unilateral obligation not undertaken in the course of a business, and a cautionary obligation will sometimes be such an obligation. Further, where the cautionary obligation amounts to a security or guarantee for a regulated agreement under the Consumer Credit Act 1974 (the "1974 Act"), s 105(1) of the 1974 Act states that it must be in writing and executed by the cautioner.

Other requirements

Subject to the above, a contract of cautionry can be constituted in the same way as any contract, that is to say by offer and acceptance. However, a general offer can be made and express acceptance is not always necessary, which is linked to the debate concerning whether cautionry is properly regarded as a contract or promise. For example, in the case of *Fortune* v *Young* (1918), the Court of Session ruled that where a cautioner gives a letter to a particular individual which makes a general offer to act as a cautioner to any third-party creditor in respect of the debts or obligations of that particular individual as debtor, that offer is valid and may be enforced by any third-party creditor duly acting on it. Furthermore, the case of *Wallace* v *Gibson* (1895) is an authority for the proposition that it is possible to constitute a cautionary obligation by the creditor acting on a cautioner's unconditional offer to give caution without the requirement for any prior acceptance on the part of the creditor before dealings are entered into with the debtor. It is also possible for there to be more than one cautioner. In such circumstances, the cautioners are known as co-cautioners.

ACCESSORY NATURE OF CAUTIONARY OBLIGATION

Introduction

A cautionary obligation is accessory in nature. Therefore, it is not an independent principal obligation which stands on its own and it cannot exist without linkage to a principal obligation between a debtor and a creditor. When the principal obligation is extinguished, so is the cautionary obligation (*Swan* v *Bank of Scotland* (1836)).

Distinction between cautionary obligation and indemnity

A particular difficulty is distinguishing a cautionary obligation from an independent principal obligation such as an indemnity. An indemnity is essentially an obligation by a party to make good a loss sustained by, or pay a sum of money to, a third party on the occurrence of a particular event. The factor which distinguishes an indemnity from a cautionary obligation is that the former is not accessory to an independent obligation to pay a principal debt. However, the problem is that sometimes the event which triggers the indemnity is the failure of a party to pay a debt to another party. In such circumstances, it is far from straightforward to ascertain the nature of the obligation to pay and whether it is an indemnity or a cautionary obligation. For example, consider a scenario where A enters into a principal obligation to pay £10,000 to B, and C agrees to pay B in the event that A does not do so. Of course, the agreement may expressly state that the obligation is a cautionary obligation or an indemnity. The difficulty is where the obligation is not specifically labelled as a cautionary obligation or an indemnity. It may not therefore be straightforward to determine whether C's obligation is a principal obligation, and thus an indemnity, rather than an accessory one, and thus a cautionary obligation. The courts have sometimes had to deal with cases concerning the distinction, and a key distinguishing factor was identified by Lord Esher MR in *Sutton & Co v Grey* (1894), who stated that where C in the above example is totally unconnected with the transaction between A and B except for their promise to pay the loss, then C's obligation will be cautionary, whereas if C is not totally unconnected with the transaction but is to derive some benefit from it (eg a commission fee), then C's obligation will be deemed to be an indemnity.

Distinction between cautionary obligation and other obligations

The case of *Stevenson's Trustee v Campbell & Sons* (1896) is an authority for the point that there is also a distinction between a cautionary obligation and an agency-type situation where Y agrees to order goods for Z on the basis that Y will pay for them. In this example, the principal obligation is imposed on Y, rather than Y acting in the capacity as cautioner for Z. Moreover, some documents which specifically state that they are guarantees are not in fact guarantees and so do not give rise to cautionary obligations, and instead create primary liability. A notable example is the performance bond or performance guarantee where, in return for a fee, a bank obliges itself to make a payment to A in the event that B fails to fulfil its obligation(s) to A (*Cargill International SA v Bangladesh Sugar and Food Industries Corporation* (1998)).

Implications of obligation being cautionary in nature

Where a primary obligation is extinguished, the cautionary obligation falls, whereas the extinction of an independent obligation does not affect the

continuance or validity of an indemnity or obligation which is not cautionary (*Yeoman Credit Ltd* v *Latter* (1961)). Thus, it is crucial to distinguish
between a cautionary obligation and an obligation that resembles a cautionary obligation but which is in fact independent in nature.

PROPER AND IMPROPER CAUTIONRY

Bell's *Principles*, s 246 directs that a contract of proper cautionry is one in which
it is evident from the express terms of the deed that a person is a cautioner.
However, in the case of a contract of improper cautionry, there is the appearance that the cautioner and the principal debtor are joint co-debtors but the
actual situation can be ascertained by eg a careful reading of the agreement or
the creditor has the relevant knowledge. Historically, the distinction was crucial since it was only a proper cautioner who was entitled to exercise the rights
of discussion and division. While the distinction retains some significance, it
has been restricted. The right of discussion is a cautioner's right to insist that
the creditor takes all reasonable steps against the debtor to enforce payment of
the debt through court action and diligence prior to seeking to enforce the
payment of the debtor's debt against the cautioner in terms of the cautionary
obligation. Section 8 of the Mercantile Law Amendment (Scotland) Act 1856,
however, removed the right of discussion, with an exception for circumstances where discussion is expressly provided for in the instrument of caution. The effect of this statutory provision is that a creditor does not ordinarily
need to "discuss" the debt before moving against the cautioner. Meanwhile,
in terms of the right of division, each co-cautioner is liable for their *pro rata*
share of the debtor's debt only and other co-cautioners must be asked to pay as
well. This can be contrasted with improper cautionry where co-cautioners are
jointly and severally liable for the principal debt.

THE EFFECT OF MISREPRESENTATION, UNDUE INFLUENCE AND FACILITY AND CIRCUMVENTION ON THE CONTRACT OF CAUTIONRY

Misrepresentation, undue influence and facility and circumvention

Where a cautionary obligation is entered into due to the creditor's misrepresentation, undue influence, facility or circumvention or force and fear,
the obligation will be voidable or void (see eg *Smith* v *Bank of Scotland*
(1829)). This reflects the fact that a contract of cautionry is governed by
general contractual principles. To allow for avoidance of the cautionary
obligation, a misrepresentation must induce the cautioner to enter into the

contract of cautionry, and requires to be material (*Royal Bank of Scotland* v *Ranken* (1844)). The rules on misrepresentation, however, do not lead to a separate rule that the creditor is under a positive duty to disclose material facts of which the cautioner was unaware, which if disclosed may have affected the cautioner's decision to enter into the cautionary obligation (*Young* v *Clydesdale Bank* (1889)). However, if any representation is made it requires to be "full and fair" (*Royal Bank of Scotland* v *O'Donnell* (2015)).

Misrepresentation by debtor to, or undue influence by debtor over, the cautioner

In the case of a misrepresentation made by the debtor to the cautioner or the exertion of undue influence on the cautioner by the debtor, historically, the legal position was that the validity of the cautionary obligation would not be called into question except in circumstances where the creditor was aware of the misrepresentation or undue influence. However, the position changed when the House of Lords decided *Smith* v *Bank of Scotland* (1997). In *Smith*, a wife claimed that she had been induced to enter into a cautionary obligation in respect of the debts of her husband's business by virtue of a misrepresentation made to her by her husband and by the exertion of undue influence. The creditor was unaware of any misrepresentation or undue influence. Nevertheless, the House of Lords ruled that the doctrine of good faith imposes an obligation on a creditor to advise a prospective cautioner to take independent legal advice where the circumstances are such that a reasonable person would believe that, owing to the personal relationship between the debtor and the prospective cautioner, the consent of the latter may not be freely given or fully informed. Where the creditor fails in the obligation to direct the cautioner to obtain independent legal advice, they are not in good faith and so the cautionary obligation cannot be enforced, assuming there has been an actionable wrong by the debtor. There may also be a requirement for a party to agree to act as cautioner gratuitously in order for them to successfully contend that the obligation is not enforceable in the circumstances. Relationships which are sufficiently close to the creditor to give rise to the "good faith" duty include husband and wife and, as shown in *Wright* v *Cotias Investments Inc* (2000), parent and child where the parent is acting as the cautioner. The same rule may also apply to other relationships, such as certain cohabiting relationships.

Content of the creditor's "good faith" obligation

With regard to the content of the creditor's obligation, *Forsyth* v *Royal Bank of Scotland* (2000) provides that if the cautioner is separately legally advised, the creditor need not take any further steps. Thus, a practice has emerged whereby the creditor will insist that the cautioner takes separate legal advice. *Broadway* v *Clydesdale Bank plc (No 1)* (2000) held that if the creditor has *reasonable grounds* for believing that such independent legal advice has been taken by the cautioner, the creditor will have no further obligation. Practical steps taken by lenders to avoid falling short of the requirements incumbent upon them mean there is a general absence of cases in which a cautioner has demonstrated a breach of the duty of good faith by a creditor (for an exception to this, see *Cooper* v *Bank of Scotland* (2014)).

THE CAUTIONER'S LIABILITY

The exposure of a cautioner in respect of their cautionary obligation is a matter of interpretation of the contract of cautionry itself. *Aitken's Trustees* v *Bank of Scotland* (1945) provides that a cautionary obligation will be construed *contra proferentem*, that is, construed in favour of the cautioner and against the creditor. Where a cautioner enters into a cautionary obligation, the case of *Jackson* v *McIver* (1875) demonstrates that the extent of their liability can never be greater than that of the debtor. However, pursuant to *Struthers* v *Dykes* (1847), the cautioner may be liable for the costs and expenses of the creditor in taking steps against the debtor to enforce the debt. Where a cautioner enters into a cautionary obligation which guarantees all of the advances to be made to a debtor but places a financial limit on the extent of that liability, the cautioner will not be liable for sums advanced by the creditor to the debtor after the date on which that financial limit is met.

Extent of caution

Caution may be continuing or limited in its scope. Where a cautionary obligation is continuing, the cautioner is liable for all sums which are outstanding by the debtor. This can be contrasted with a limited cautionary obligation where the cautioner's exposure is limited to a particular transaction or series of transactions. Whether a cautionary obligation is continuing or limited is a matter of interpretation of the relevant contract (*Caledonian Banking Co* v *Kennedy's Trustees* (1870)).

THE CAUTIONER'S RIGHTS

Cautioners have a right of relief, the right to demand an assignation of the rights under the debt from the creditor, the right to share in any security granted by the debtor to a co-cautioner and the right to rank in the bankruptcy or sequestration of the debtor's estate where the cautioner has paid the creditor in full.

Right of relief

The right of relief entitles the cautioner to demand that the principal debtor relieve them of all liability incurred to the creditor. Where the contract is silent as to an express right of relief, Erskine, *Institute*, III, 3, 65 stipulates that the right will be implied as a consequence of the *actio mandati* which the cautioner has against the principal debtor. The right of relief also extends to the expenses which the cautioner incurred in paying the principal debt and interest paid to the creditor (*Smithy's Place Ltd v Blackadder* (1991)). The right of relief is also available where the debt is not yet due and the cautioner has not been called upon by the creditor to pay the principal debt (*Doig v Lawrie* (1903)).

Right of assignation

The cautioner's right of assignation, which is known as the *beneficium cedendarum actionum*, enables the cautioner to call on the creditor to assign the debt and any securities for it, including diligences done by the creditor. However, the *beneficium cedendarum actionum* does not apply to securities granted to the creditor by third parties (*Gordon's Trustees v Young* (1910)). This right is available to the cautioner once they have paid the principal debt in full and ensures that the cautioner steps into the shoes of the creditor. The purpose of this right is to enable the cautioner to enforce their right of relief against the debtor or against co-cautioners.

Right to share in security

The cautioner's right to share in any security granted by the debtor to a co-cautioner is also useful, allowing all cautioners to benefit from such a security without a preference being allocated by the creditor, but like the *beneficium cedendarum actionum* does not apply to securities granted by third parties (*Scott v Young* (1909)).

Right to rank in insolvency

Where the principal debtor becomes bankrupt and the cautioner pays the creditor in full, the cautioner will rank in the insolvency of the debtor as an ordinary creditor. Difficulties arise where the extent of the cautioner's liability extends to part only of the principal debt or where the caution is for the whole debt but a limitation has been placed on the amount for which it is to be liable, and a larger debt has been incurred. Much depends on the construction of the contract since, in the case of the former, the cautioner will be entitled to rank in respect of sums paid by the cautioner up to the limit, whereas, in the latter situation, the cautioner will not be entitled to rank.

TERMINATION OF THE CAUTIONARY OBLIGATION BY EXTINCTION OF THE PRINCIPAL DEBT

Since a cautionary obligation is accessory in nature, where the principal obligation is extinguished, the cautionary obligation is also extinguished. Thus, the cautioner's obligation is extinguished where the principal debtor is discharged from liability by the creditor without the cautioner's consent (*Aitken's Trustees* v *Bank of Scotland* (1945)).

Extinction by novation

A cautionary obligation may also be extinguished by the novation of the principal debt. Novation occurs where the principal debt is terminated and a new debt is constituted, that is, one obligation is substituted for another. Where the identity of the principal debtor changes, that is, the party owing the obligation is changed, the cautioner is released from their cautionary obligation. Novation is distinct from assignation since, in the case of an assignation, the obligation is one and the same and it is only the identity of the creditor which changes. In the case of assignation, the cautioner continues to be bound by their cautionary obligation (*Waydale Ltd* v *DHL Holdings (UK) Ltd (No 2)* (2001)).

Extinction by compensation or prescription

The exercise of compensation may also function to relieve a cautioner of their obligation. If the creditor is due money to the cautioner or the debtor when the creditor makes a demand against the cautioner for the payment of the principal debt, the operation of compensation may result in the extinction of the cautioner's obligation. Prescription of the principal obligation will also result in the extinction of the cautionary obligation.

Clayton's Case

In the context of a current account, the rule in *Clayton's Case* (*Devaynes* v *Noble, Clayton's Case* (1816)) may operate to extinguish the cautioner's liability. This rule provides that in the case of a current account between debtor and creditor, when a payment is made to account and there has been no appropriation of the payment by either the debtor or the creditor, the law will stipulate that payments to the credit side are applied to reduce items on the debit side in the chronological order in which they were incurred. When this rule is applied, the consequence is that the principal debt that has been guaranteed may be extinguished, with the outcome that the cautioner is discharged.

TERMINATION OF THE CAUTIONARY OBLIGATION BY THE ACTIONS OF THE CREDITOR

The creditor's actions may be such that the law presumes that the cautioner is released from its cautionary obligation. There are certain well-recognised categories where the actions of the creditor are deemed to be consistent with such an intention to release the cautioner.

"Giving time"

The first category arises where the creditor "gives time" to the principal without the consent of the cautioner (*C & A Johnstone* v *Duthie* (1892)). The creditor will be deemed to have given the debtor time where the creditor agrees to postpone the time at which payment by the principal debtor is due.

Prejudicial alteration of contract between debtor and creditor

Second, the cautioner will be discharged if they are prejudiced, without their consent, by an alteration of the contract between the creditor and the principal debtor. For example, in the case of *N G Napier Ltd* v *Crosbie* (1964), the cautioner was released from liability where the principal debtor's weekly repayments of the principal were increased.

Discharge of co-cautioner

Third, s 9 of the Mercantile Law Amendment (Scotland) Act 1856 directs that a joint cautioner will be discharged where the creditor discharges another joint co-cautioner without the consent of the joint cautioner. This section does not apply where the cautioner is not jointly liable with the co-cautioner and where both parties have guaranteed to repay a separate sum. A good example is the case of *Morgan* v *Smart* (1872) where a co-cautioner was liable for £70 of a guaranteed debt of £105. The cautioner was liable to the extent of £35 where the co-cautioner had paid £70 and been discharged by the creditor.

Giving up of security

Finally, a cautioner will be discharged where the creditor voluntarily gives up a security by releasing the cautioner to the value of that security.

TERMINATION OF THE CAUTIONARY OBLIGATION BY THE CAUTIONER AND BY OPERATION OF LAW

No unilateral revocation

The general rule is that a cautioner is not entitled to be released from their cautionary obligation by unilateral revocation if they are guaranteeing a specific obligation. However, where the guarantee is continuing and no period of time is specified, *Buchanan* v *Main* (1900) demonstrates that the cautioner may, in the absence of an express provision precluding revocation, withdraw as to future advances by giving notice to the creditor.

Operation of express term

A cautionary obligation may also terminate by operation of the express terms of the contract: for example, where the guarantee is for a fixed term or for a specific transaction only, the expiry of that fixed term or the completion of that transaction will discharge the cautioner in respect of future liabilities to the creditor.

Death of debtor or creditor

Moreover, the death of the debtor or the creditor will discharge the cautioner from performance in respect of future advances. However, the cautioner will remain liable for existing sums due. If the cautioner dies, this does not discharge them from performance. Their executor will be liable to make good the cautionary obligation.

Prescription

Finally, a cautionary obligation may be extinguished by prescription in terms of s 6(1)–(3) of the Prescription and Limitation (Scotland) Act 1973 where 5 years have elapsed since it became enforceable and no relevant claim or no acknowledgement of the existence of the obligation has been made during that period.

Essential Facts

- A contract of cautionry will provide that the cautioner will pay a certain sum of money (usually the principal debt, plus interest on that sum and the creditor's costs and expenses) or perform a particular obligation in the event that the principal debtor fails to pay such sum or perform such obligation.
- A cautionary obligation is accessory to the principal obligation in the sense that its enforceability rests on the principal obligation of the principal debtor.
- Subject to s 1(2)(a)(ii) of the Requirements of Writing (Scotland) Act 1995 and s 105(1) of the Consumer Credit Act 1974, cautionary obligations do not require to be committed to writing in order to be validly constituted.
- A contract of cautionry can be constituted by offer and acceptance; however, a general offer to act as cautioner can be made and express acceptance is not always necessary.
- A cautionary obligation is distinct from an indemnity, the latter being an independent primary obligation.
- Where a primary obligation is extinguished, the cautionary obligation falls.
- A cautionary obligation may be proper or improper.
- The doctrine of good faith imposes an obligation on a creditor to advise a prospective cautioner to take independent legal advice where the circumstances are such that a reasonable person would believe that, owing to the personal relationship between the debtor and the prospective cautioner, the consent of the latter may not be freely given or fully informed. Where this duty has been breached by the creditor and the debtor has committed an actionable wrong against the cautioner, the cautionary obligation may be unenforceable.
- A cautionary obligation will be construed *contra proferentem*, ie in favour of the cautioner and against the creditor.
- Cautioners have a right of relief, the right to demand an assignation from the creditor, the right to share in any security granted by the debtor to a co-cautioner and the right to rank in the debtor's insolvency where the cautioner has paid the creditor in full.
- A cautionary obligation may be extinguished by the actions of the creditor, by the cautioner (for future advances) or by operation of law.

Essential Cases

Fortune v Young (1918): where a cautioner gives a letter to a particular individual which makes a general offer to act as a cautioner to any third-party creditor in respect of the debts or obligations of that particular individual as debtor, that offer amounts to a cautionary obligation when acted upon.

Wallace v Gibson (1895): a cautionary obligation may be constituted by the creditor acting on a cautioner's unconditional offer to give caution without the requirement for any prior acceptance on the part of the creditor before dealings are entered into with the debtor.

Swan v Bank of Scotland (1836): when the principal obligation is extinguished, so is the cautionary obligation.

Sutton & Co v Grey (1894): identifies a means for distinguishing between a cautionary obligation and an independent obligation (for example, an indemnity).

Cargill International SA v Bangladesh Sugar and Food Industries Corp (1998): a performance bond or performance guarantee is not a cautionary obligation.

Royal Bank of Scotland v Ranken (1844): to allow for avoidance of the cautionary obligation, a misrepresentation must induce the cautioner to enter into the contract of cautionry and must be material.

Smith v Bank of Scotland (1997): the doctrine of good faith imposes an obligation on a creditor to advise a prospective cautioner to take independent legal advice where the circumstances are such that a reasonable person would believe that, owing to the personal relationship between the debtor and the prospective cautioner, the consent of the latter may not be freely given or fully informed.

Broadway v Clydesdale Bank plc (No 1) (2000): if the creditor has *reasonable grounds* to believe that the cautioner has taken independent legal advice, the creditor will have no further obligation in order to discharge its duties under *Smith* v *Bank of Scotland* (1997).

Aitken's Trustees v Bank of Scotland (1945): (1) a cautionary obligation will be construed *contra proferentem*; and (2) the cautioner's obligation is extinguished where the principal debtor is discharged from liability by the creditor without the cautioner's consent.

Jackson v McIver (1875): the cautioner's liability can never be greater than that of the debtor.

C & A Johnstone v Duthie (1892): where the creditor "gives time" to the principal debtor without the consent of the cautioner, this may extinguish the cautionary obligation.

N G Napier Ltd v Crosbie (1964): the cautioner will be discharged from their cautionary obligation if they are prejudiced, without their consent, by an alteration of the contract between the creditor and the principal debtor.

7 FORMS OF PAYMENT

Commercial activity depends upon the provision of goods and services and parties are only likely to offer these in return for satisfactory payment. Sometimes a party will want immediate payment or consideration in return for goods or services, while in other cases one party incurs a debt to another by contractual agreement, including in the context of a loan that will need to be repaid. Debt and its counterpart, credit, are vital in a modern commercial society and the law needs to determine how debts can be satisfied. This chapter will consider available forms of payment used to fulfil obligations and satisfy debts and will then move on to examine a complicated and traditionally important payment mechanism that is still sometimes included in commercial law curricula, namely bills of exchange.

PAYMENT

In the context of a contract, parties incur obligations to perform. The performance may involve providing a service, such as accountancy advice or cleaning work, or the transfer of ownership of goods or land or other property. In return for such performance a party will ordinarily seek performance from the contractual counterparty in the form of monetary payment. However, it is possible that the counter performance could instead be the provision of services or the transfer of property. This depends on what has been contractually agreed by the parties: it is up to them to agree what they are willing to accept by way of payment.

Money and payment

Usually payment is associated with money but the meaning of the term "money" depends on the context. It is most often identified as cash in the form of notes and coins; however, in commercial scenarios the significance of this type of money is relatively limited and is becoming increasingly less important. This has been accelerated, including for consumer transactions, by the COVID-19 pandemic. Most money is incorporeal (intangible) and is held in bank accounts. In technical terms, money in a bank account is a debt that the bank owes to the account holder, unless, for example, the account holder has entered their overdraft, in which case they owe the amount in question as a debt to the bank. The majority of payments nowadays consist of electronic funds transfers involving bank accounts. If a party wishes to buy an item or a service, they will usually "transfer" funds from their own account to the account of the seller. In legal terms, however, this is not a transfer or assignation in the usual sense. Instead, the payment means that the debt owed by the bank to the purchaser, in terms of their bank account, is reduced or wiped out and the debt owed by the seller's bank to the seller, in terms of their account, is increased correspondingly. Consequently, once payment is made, the seller's right to receive the money will be against their own bank rather than against the purchaser.

Legal tender

As noted already, it is up to the parties to determine the form of payment required. However, subject to that, certain types of payment are accepted as unchallengeable means of satisfying debts: this is what is known as "legal tender" (a party cannot be sued for non-payment if they make payment using legal tender). In *Glasgow Pavilion Ltd* v *Motherwell* (1903), Lord Young stated that a creditor is not required to receive payment of a debt due "by cheque or otherwise than in the current coin of the realm" and added that a creditor can even refuse Scottish bank notes. While three Scottish banks have the ability to issue banknotes, these are not legal tender. Under section 1 of the Currency and Bank Notes Act 1954 any banknotes issued by the Bank of England are legal tender in England and Wales but will only be legal tender in Scotland if their value is less than five pounds and there are no longer any notes issued for such a value. Section 2 of the Coinage Act 1971 specifies the coins that are legal tender. Gold coins are legal tender for payment of any amount, as are other coins such as one pound and two pound coins by separate provision. Coins of cupro-nickel or silver of more than 10 pence (such as 20p and 50p coins) can be used for payment of any amount up to £10. Coins of cupro-nickel or silver of 10 pence and under can be used for payment of any amount up to £5. Finally, bronze coins can be used for payment of debt up to 20 pence. In reality of course very few commercial transactions will involve one party having to use legal tender to fulfil their debt obligation(s).

Cryptocurrencies

A relatively new form of payment that has increased in prominence and significance in recent years is cryptocurrency. There are many different cryptocurrencies available such as Bitcoin and the market for such assets is expanding and often volatile. Cryptocurrencies serve various purposes, including as a form of investment, and they can be used for payment if the counterparty is willing to accept them. Thus, a cryptocurrency can either be purchased as an asset, or it can be used as consideration to obtain an asset or service in some circumstances. A cryptocurrency is a type of privately issued digital asset. It is not a currency in a strict sense, albeit that some central banks, such as the Bank of England, are proposing to create their own digital currencies. Even though it is not possible here to explain technical details regarding cryptocurrencies in any detail, it can be noted that they rely upon digital ledgers with discrete data entries constituting units of the cryptocurrency.

Cryptocurrencies are a sub-category of cryptoassets, and while there is no single definition of cryptocurrency or cryptoasset applicable in all contexts, "cryptoasset" is defined in a statutory instrument relating to money laundering and terrorist financing as "a cryptographically secured digital representation of value or contractual rights that uses a form of distributed ledger technology and can be transferred, stored or traded electronically" (Money Laundering, Terrorist Financing and Transfer of Funds (Information on the Payer) Regulations 2017 (SI 2017/692), reg 14A(3), as inserted by the Money Laundering and Terrorist Financing (Amendment) Regulations 2019 (SI 2019/1511)). As a novel form of asset, the nature of cryptocurrencies is still somewhat uncertain. However, they are increasingly being recognised in English law as a form of intangible property (see eg *AA* v *Persons Unknown* (2019)) and it can be expected that they will be accepted as a form of incorporeal moveable property in Scots law. The holder of a cryptocurrency unit has the ability to transfer it and may be able to create other property rights in relation to it, and it will likely be treated as property in contexts such as insolvency law.

Other payment mechanisms

As well as the types of payment noted above, various other payment mechanisms can be used by parties in transactions to fulfil debt obligations (if the parties agree). These include payment by debit card, which involves a purchaser using a card issued by their bank to execute payment from their own bank account to the seller's bank account and is a version of the electronic "transfer" of funds mentioned previously. Direct debits and standing orders also consist of electronic payments, with instructions given to make regular payments from a party's account. While the payment amounts for standing orders are fixed, this does not have to be the case for direct debits. Credit cards share some similarities with debit cards but involve a pre-arranged credit limit which the credit card company extends to the card holder; and, if the card holder uses the card for a purchase, they require to repay the amount incurred in accordance with the agreed terms (and this may include interest and charges). Further details about credit cards and certain other forms of payment are provided in Chapter 8 on Consumer Credit. It can be added here that a store card is a type of credit card issued by a certain retailer and can only be spent on purchases from that retailer, but they often entitle their holder to discounts and other benefits. Vouchers and gift cards are pre-paid with a monetary value and can be redeemed to purchase items or services at a specific retailer or group of retailers. Having now already discussed a number of different forms of payment, in the next section a significant category of instrument that entitles its holder to payment, namely a negotiable instrument, will be considered in detail.

NEGOTIABLE INSTRUMENTS

A negotiable instrument confers a right in favour of the owner to the payment of a sum of money. The amount of money is represented on the face of the document and so it is representative of a right of the owner of the instrument to be paid a debt from a third party. Ownership of the bill/document is transferred by indorsement and delivery or, in the case of some documents, delivery only. While negotiable instruments take the form of paper documents, there are proposals to allow for certain negotiable instruments including bills of exchange and promissory notes (as well as other trade documents) to exist in electronic form and such reforms may extend to Scots law.

Negotiability

The key matter which distinguishes the negotiable instrument from other forms of incorporeal moveable property representing a right to be paid a debt (a negotiable instrument is a form of incorporeal moveable property) is that the *nemo dat quod non habet* and *tantum et tale* rules do not apply where the transferee of the negotiable instrument pays value for the document and is in good faith. Rather than being transferred by assignation, a negotiable instrument is transferred by negotiation. Negotiability is extremely beneficial to a transferee. Once the instrument is transferred for value by A to B, provided B is in good faith, the effect of transfer by negotiation is that B will take the instrument free from any defects or flaws in A's title to the instrument. Hence, in terms of the legal concept of negotiation, B will take a better title to the instrument than A had at the point of transfer. This can be contrasted with the transfer of a debt from A to B by assignation. In such circumstances, even where B pays value to A and takes title to be paid the debt from A in good faith, any rights or defences which third parties, including the account debtor (ie the party due to pay the debt to A), have against A will also be good against B after the assignation.

Differences in transfer by negotiation and assignation

Another key difference between transfer by negotiation and assignation is that in the case of the former there is no requirement for (1) intimation of the transfer of the debt from A to B to be made to the account debtor or (2) a separate document of transfer (*Connal & Co* v *Loder* (1868)). Negotiation is what distinguishes a negotiable instrument from other property which establishes the right to be paid a debt. For example, a contractual right to be paid a debt pursuant to a bill of lading (*Kum* v *Wah Tat Bank* (1971)), an IOU (*Muir* v *Muir* (1912)) and a building society withdrawal form (*Weir* v *National Westminster Bank* (1994)) are not negotiable instruments, since the sums of money represented by such pieces of paper are not transferable by indorsement and delivery, nor do they confer a better title on the transferee than that wielded by the transferor. The most common well-recognised forms of negotiable instrument are bills of exchange, cheques, sterling paper notes, promissory notes, bankers' drafts and Government Treasury bills. The focus for the remainder of this chapter will be on bills of exchange, a particularly important form of negotiable instrument (especially historically) and from which much can be learnt about negotiable instruments more generally.

BILLS OF EXCHANGE

Introduction

A bill of exchange is a form of negotiable instrument developed by commercial merchants in Medieval Europe. Instead of carrying cash and notes long distances, bills of exchange could be carried across borders and drawn on banks in different cities across Europe, whereupon the banks would make payment to the holder of the negotiable instrument in terms of the instructions on the bill itself. The beauty of the bill is that it could be transferred to a third party by negotiation as well as drawn on an identified bank. Originally, bills of exchange were regulated by the *lex mercatoria* (law merchant). However, the law governing bills of exchange is now found in the Bills of Exchange Act 1882 (the "1882 Act"). Note that in terms of s 73 of the 1882 Act, cheques are bills of exchange drawn on a banker payable on demand. Thus, cheques can be considered a special type of bill of exchange. More generally, bills of exchange continue to have particular significance in relation to international trade. For example, they circumvent some of the difficulties concerning the sale of goods involving parties operating in different jurisdictions, including minimising the risk of non-payment by the purchaser.

Identity of parties

Within the 1882 Act, the relevant parties are referred to as the drawer, drawee, payee and indorsee. The drawer is the party who issues the bill and orders the drawee to make payment to the payee or the indorsee. The payee is the party in whose favour the bill is initially drawn and the drawee is the party on whom the bill is drawn and who is instructed by the drawer to pay the payee. So, for example, if the Bank of Belgium issues a bill of exchange to Joanna instructing the Bank of Perthshire to pay Joanna £10,000 on the presentation of the bill, the Bank of Belgium is the drawer, the Bank of Perthshire the drawee and Joanna is the payee. The drawee (ie the Bank of Perthshire) accepts liability on the bill by signing the front of the bill when it is presented by Joanna and then paying over the requisite sum of money to Joanna. At this point, the drawee (ie the Bank of Perthshire) becomes the acceptor. If Joanna sells the bill to Didier by indorsing ("indorsation") and delivering it (ie she negotiates the bill in favour of Didier) to Didier before it is presented to the drawee (ie the Bank of Perthshire), Didier will become the indorsee. Indorsation is achieved by the payee signing the back of the bill of exchange in favour of the indorsee: for example, when Didier pays Joanna a sum of money representing the sum stated on the bill (usually at a discount), Joanna will then sign over the bill to Didier by indorsing her signature on the back of the bill and naming Didier as the indorsee. Didier then has the option to present the bill to the Bank of Perthshire or do the same as Joanna and indorse the bill on to another third party in return for payment. In this way, bills of exchange may be transferred a number of times before finally being drawn on the drawee.

Definition of "bill of exchange"

Section 3(1) of the 1882 Act defines a "bill of exchange" as "an unconditional order in writing, addressed by one person to another, signed by the person giving it, requiring the person to whom it is addressed to pay on demand or at a fixed or determinable future time a sum certain in money to or to the order of a specified person, or to bearer". Each of these components must be satisfied in order for a document to qualify as a bill of exchange. It is worth noting that there is no requirement for the bill to be dated when it is issued. Each of the individual elements of the definition in s 3(1) of the 1882 Act will now be considered.

An "unconditional order"

First, the document must amount to "an unconditional order" on its face. The words "please pay" are satisfactory, but "we hereby authorise you to pay" in the case of *Hamilton* v *Spottiswoode* (1849) did not satisfy the definition.

Writing

Second, the unconditional order must be made "in writing". Section 2 of the 1882 Act directs that "written" includes printed and "writing" includes print. In the case of *Geary* v *Physic* (1826), it was ruled that a bill may be validly drawn up in pencil. It is not particularly common, but possible, for a bill to take up more than one page, as long as it is a single instrument (*KHR Financings Ltd* v *Jackson* (1977)). Another point is that the bill does not need to be written in the English language (*Arab Bank* v *Ross* (1952)).

Addressed by one person to another

Third, the order must be addressed by one person to another. The import of that requirement is that the order must be addressed by the drawer to the drawee. By virtue of s 6(2) of the 1882 Act, there is scope for there to be two or more drawees.

Signed by the person giving it

Fourth, the bill must be signed by the person giving it, that is, it must be signed by the drawer. The common practice is for the drawer to sign the bill in its bottom right-hand corner, but this is not an absolute requirement. Section 18(1) of the 1882 Act stipulates that a bill may be accepted by the drawee before it has been signed by the drawer or while it is otherwise incomplete. However, there is nothing in s 18(1) of the 1882 Act which compels a drawee to accept liability on a bill which has not been signed by the drawer (*McCall* v *Taylor* (1865)). By virtue of s 23(1) of the 1882 Act, it is provided that no person is liable as drawer, indorser or acceptor of a bill who has not signed it as such. However, there are two exceptions. First, where a person signs a bill in a trade or assumed name, they are liable thereon as if they had signed it in their own name. Second, the signature of the name of a firm is equivalent to the signature by the person so signing of the names of all persons liable as partners in that firm. Moreover, in terms of s 24 of the 1882 Act, a forged signature on a bill is deemed to be wholly inoperative unless the party whose signature it purports to be has given their authority. Finally, s 91(1) of the 1882 Act is to the effect that it is not necessary that a person should sign it with their own hand, but that it is sufficient if their signature is written by some other person by or under their authority, for example an agent.

Payable on demand

Fifth, the bill must be payable on demand or at a fixed or determinable future time. In terms of s 10(1) of the 1882 Act, if no time for payment is expressed on the bill, it is deemed to be payable on demand. Moreover, that section also directs that a bill is deemed to be payable on demand if it states that it is payable on sight or on presentation. If it is accepted or indorsed when it is overdue, it is deemed to be a bill payable on demand. Payment may also be in the future provided that the future event is certain to happen: for example, on the death of the drawer, which will be valid (see *Roffey* v *Greenwell* (1839)). However, if it is uncertain that the event will occur, then the bill will not be valid in terms of s 11 of the 1882 Act.

A sum certain in money

Sixth, the sum payable must amount to a sum certain in money. Section 9(1) provides further guidance, directing that payments may be made in instalments. It is also acceptable that the bill provides for the payment of interest in terms of s 9(1) of the 1882 Act. If the rate of interest is unspecified, in English law, the bill is treated as valid in terms of the case of *Re Tillman* (1918) and 5 per cent is deemed to be the appropriate rate, but there is Scottish authority in *Lamberton* v *Aiken* (1899) to the effect that such a bill would be invalid. In accordance with s 9 of the 1882 Act, interest is deemed to run from the date of the bill or, if the bill is undated, from the issue thereof.

Made to the order of a specified person or to bearer

Seventh, the bill must be made to the order of a specified person with reasonable certainty or to the bearer in terms of s 7(1) of the 1882 Act (see *Adam Associates (Strathclyde) Ltd* v *CGU Insurance plc* (2001)). The bill may be made payable to more than one person jointly or in the alternative. It may also be expressed to be payable to a person holding a particular office and if the specified person does not exist or is fictitious the bill is treated as being payable to the bearer (see s 7(3) of the 1882 Act and *Clutton & Co* v *Attenborough & Son* (1897)).

The two categories of bill of exchange

It is implicit in the definition above in s 3(1) of the 1882 Act that there are two forms of bill of exchange: first, the specified payee bill, where a particular person is named as the person entitled to payment from the drawee on the bill, be it the original payee or a subsequent indorsee; and, second, the bearer bill, where the holder of the bill is entitled to payment, whomsoever that person may be. As expressed above, a specified payee bill and/or a bearer bill may be transferred by "negotiation", that is, this is the method of transfer of such instruments. In terms of s 31(2) of the 1882 Act, a bearer bill is negotiated by delivery only. In the case of a specified payee bill, s 31(3) of the 1882 Act provides that negotiation is conducted by indorsement and delivery whereby the payee or indorsee indorses the bill and delivers it over to a subsequent indorsee in return for payment. Hence, there is a crucial difference in the method of negotiation, depending on whether the bill is payable to the bearer or is payable to a specified payee. However, in each case, delivery of the bill is crucial: s 21(1) of the 1882 Act. Therefore, although A may draw up a bill in favour of B, he is not liable on it until it is delivered to B. Likewise, if B indorses the bill to C, she will not be liable to C until it is delivered to C.

Indorsement: specified payee bill

In the context of a specified payee bill, s 32 of the 1882 Act regulates how indorsement must take place. First, an indorsement must be written on the bill itself and be signed by the indorser and the simple signature of the indorser on the bill, without additional words, is sufficient. The entire value of the bill must be indorsed and so the indorsement of only part of the amount payable on the face of the bill, or which purports to transfer the bill to two or more indorsees severally, does not operate to negotiate the bill. Where the payee or indorsee is wrongly designated on the bill or their name is spelled incorrectly, that person may indorse the bill as described on the bill and add their proper signature. Where a person indorses a bill, s 55(2) of the 1882 Act directs that that person becomes conditionally liable to subsequent indorsers or holders in the event that the bill is dishonoured. However, that person may avoid liability by writing "without recourse" alongside their signature.

The "holder" of a bill

Only holders of a bill may negotiate it. Section 2 of the 1882 Act directs that a "holder" means the payee or indorsee of a bill who is possessor of it or the bearer of the bill (in the case of a bearer bill). The 1882 Act recognises two types of holders and there is a presumption that every holder is a "holder in due course" by virtue of s 30(2) of the 1882 Act.

Holder for value

A "holder for value" is someone who at any time has given value for the bill and that person is deemed to be a holder for value as regards the acceptor and all persons who became parties to the bill prior to value being given. A holder for value has certain rights under the 1882 Act and can enforce the bill against such persons, but the "holder in due course" has the full panoply of rights available under the 1882 Act.

Holder in due course

A "holder in due course" is a person who (1) has taken a bill complete and regular on the face of it, (2) became the holder of the bill before it became due for payment and without notice of it being dishonoured in any way, (3) took the bill in good faith and for value, and (4) when the bill was negotiated to them, had no notice of any defect in the title of the person who negotiated it (s 29(1) of the 1882 Act). Section 2 of the 1882 Act states that "value" means valuable consideration and, in terms of s 90 of the 1882 Act, a matter is done in "good faith" if it is in fact done honestly, whether it is done negligently or not. The case of *Jones* v *Gordon* (1877) is authority for the proposition that a person will not be in good faith where they have a suspicion that something is wrong but make no enquiry for fear of what will be uncovered. The effect of being a holder in due course is spelled out in s 38(2) of the 1882 Act, which provides that the holder in due course holds the bill free from any defect in title of prior parties, as well as from personal defences available to prior parties among themselves, and may enforce payment against all parties liable on the bill. Thus, the holder in due course may enforce the bill even where it has been stolen or prior transactions between indorsees have been subject to fraud (*Whistler* v *Forster* (1863)). Thus, it is the holder in due course, rather than the holder for value, who enjoys the full beneficial effects of negotiability.

Liability on a bill

Sections 53–58 of the 1882 Act govern who will be liable on a bill of exchange and in what order such liability will attach. Obviously, the person one might initially think would be liable on a bill is the drawee, since the bill is drawn as an order on the drawee to make payment to the payee or indorsee. However, a drawee will only be liable on a bill when they accept liability on the bill; and, where they refuse to accept such liability, they may be liable directly to the drawer who drew up the bill (*Hopkinson* v *Forster* (1874)).

"Funds attached" rule

By virtue of s 53(2) of the 1882 Act, where the drawee of a bill has in their hands funds available for the payment of the sum on the bill, the bill operates as an assignment of the sum for which it is drawn in favour of the holder, from the time when the bill is presented to the drawee. The effect of this subsection is that, on the presentation of the bill, the holder has the right to be paid any sum standing to the credit of the drawer which is held by the drawee up to the amount of the bill. This is shown by the case of *British Linen Bank v Carruthers* (1883) where the holder of a cheque for £161 presented it to the bank for payment. The bank rejected the cheque on the basis that the customer (who, of course, was the drawer of the bill) had only £136 in his account with the bank. The customer/drawer went bankrupt and the trustee in bankruptcy appointed over the estate of the customer/drawer claimed the £136 in the customer's account from the bank. However, the holder of the cheque who had presented it to the bank claimed that the £136 belonged to him on the basis that s 53(2) of the 1882 Act operated to assign the funds of the drawer held by the drawee to him. The court agreed with the holder. However, it must be stressed that the "funds attached" rule in s 53(2) of the 1882 Act no longer applies to cheques (ie it applies to bills of exchange only) presented for payment by virtue of an amendment contained in s 254(4) of the Banking Act 2009.

Liability and duties of the acceptor

Section 54 of the 1882 Act regulates the liability of the acceptor on a bill by providing that when the acceptor accepts a bill, they undertake to pay it according to the tenor of their acceptance. Section 54(2) directs that the acceptor is precluded from denying to a holder in due course (1) the existence of the drawer, the genuineness of his signature and his capacity and authority to draw the bill, (2) in the case of a bill payable to drawer's order, the then capacity of the drawer to indorse, but not the genuineness or validity of his indorsement, and (3) in the case of a bill payable to the order of a third person, the existence of the payee and his then capacity to indorse, but not the genuineness or validity of his indorsement. However, it should be recalled that an acceptor is permitted to refuse payment on the bill by virtue of the fact that an indorsement is a forgery.

Enforcement against persons other than drawee

If the drawee dishonours the bill, s 55(1) of the 1882 Act enables the holder to enforce it against the drawer. By drawing up a bill, a drawer undertakes that on due presentment it shall be accepted and paid according to its tenor, and that if it is dishonoured the drawer will compensate the holder or any indorser who is compelled to pay it. The drawer is also precluded from denying to a holder in due course the existence of the payee and their then capacity to indorse. The effect of s 55(1) is that a drawer will have (1) primary liability on

a bill if it is dishonoured by the drawee and/or (2) secondary liability on a bill
if it is accepted by the drawee but payment is not made to the holder.

Enforcement against indorser

Where neither the drawee nor the drawer accepts liability on the bill, the
holder will be entitled to seek payment from an indorser on the bill. By
indorsing a bill, an indorser does three things under s 55(2) of the 1882 Act.
First, the indorser undertakes that on due presentment it shall be accepted
and paid, and that if it is dishonoured he will compensate the holder or a
subsequent indorser who is compelled to pay it. Second, the indorser is
precluded from denying to a holder in due course the genuineness and
regularity in all respects of the drawer's signature and all previous indorse-
ments. Finally, the indorser is precluded from denying to his immediate or
a subsequent indorsee that the bill was at the time of his indorsement a valid
and subsisting bill, and that he had then a good title thereto.

Discharge

Where a bill is presented and honoured by the drawee, acceptor, drawer
or indorser, the bill is said to be "discharged", that is, paid and honoured.
Discharge can be contrasted with "dishonour", which arises where the bill
is presented but not honoured by the drawee, etc.

Method of enforcement

A bill may be enforced in a number of ways. Most bills of exchange will be
payable by the drawee on demand. In such a case, a bill which is expressed
to be payable on demand will be enforced on the sight of the drawee or
on presentation to the drawee. The effect of s 10(1) of the 1882 Act is that
a bill which states that it is payable on demand, on sight or on presentation
is duly deemed to be payable on demand. Where a bill is not so expressed,
then, in terms of s 39 of the 1882 Act, the bill must be presented to the
drawee for acceptance. In terms of s 39, a bill must be presented for
acceptance in three circumstances. First, where a bill expressly stipulates
that it must be presented for acceptance, it must be so presented – even
in circumstances where the bill is expressed to be payable on demand.
Second, a bill must be presented for acceptance where it is drawn payable
elsewhere than the residence or place of business of the drawee. Third, a
bill must be presented for acceptance where it is drawn payable at a certain
period after sight. In the latter case, presentment for acceptance plays the
part of determining the date of maturity (ie the date of payment) of the
bill and the bill must be presented or negotiated within a reasonable time.

Presentment

Section 41 provides various rules on the method for the presentment of bills. First, presentment must be made by or on behalf of the holder to the drawee or to some person authorised to accept or refuse acceptance on their behalf at a reasonable hour on a business day and before the bill is overdue. Second, where the drawee is dead, presentment may be made to their personal representative, that is, their executor. Where the drawee is bankrupt, presentment may be made to them or to their trustee in sequestration.

Presentment excused

Section 41(2) of the 1882 Act provides for situations where presentment for acceptance is excused and a bill may be treated as dishonoured for acceptance. First, such presentment is not necessary where the drawee is dead or bankrupt, or is a fictitious person or a person not having capacity to contract by bill. Second, the same applies where such presentment cannot be effected after the exercise of reasonable diligence. Third, presentment is excused where, although the presentment has been irregular, acceptance has been refused on some other ground. Nevertheless, in terms of s 41(3) of the 1882 Act, the fact that the holder has reason to believe that the bill, on presentment, will be dishonoured does not excuse presentment.

Non-acceptance

Sections 42 and 43 of the 1882 Act govern the situation where a bill which must be presented for acceptance is not accepted by the parties stipulated in s 41. Sections 42 and 43 provide that "non-acceptance" is deemed to have occurred where a bill is presented for acceptance but is not accepted (ie acceptance is refused or cannot be obtained, or the bill is excused from presentment or acceptance and is not accepted) within the customary time. At that point, the holder must treat it as dishonoured, and, if the holder fails to treat it so, they lose their right of recourse against the drawer and the indorsers. If the holder does so treat the bill as dishonoured for non-acceptance, they enjoy a right of recourse against the drawer and indorsers and no presentment for payment is required.

Presentment for payment

Once the bill has been presented for acceptance, the holder must present the bill for payment, unless presentment for payment is excused. If the bill is not presented for payment, the drawer and indorser are released from liability in terms of s 45 of the 1882 Act. Where the bill is dishonoured by non-acceptance or by non-payment and a notice of dishonour is given to the drawer and each indorser in accordance with s 48 of the 1882 Act, the holder is entitled to claim against those parties.

Consumer credit

In terms of s 123 of the Consumer Credit Act 1974, a creditor may not take a negotiable instrument (other than a bank note or a cheque) to discharge any sum payable by the debtor or their cautioner under a regulated agreement. Consumer credit is considered in more detail in the next chapter.

Essential Facts

- Parties to a contract can agree what form of payment they are willing to accept.
- Payment is usually monetary and can be in the form of cash; however, most money nowadays is incorporeal and payment is normally by electronic "transfer".
- The term "legal tender" has a technical meaning and consists of the types of payment (principally involving coins) accepted as the means of satisfying debts, in the absence of contrary agreement.
- A cryptocurrency is a type of privately issued digital asset and is both a type of commodity or investment which may be considered as property and, if parties agree, can be used as a form of payment.
- A negotiable instrument confers a right in favour of the owner to the payment of a sum of money, which is specified on the face of the document and is representative of a right to be paid a debt from a third party.
- Ownership of the bill/document is transferred by indorsement and delivery or, in the case of some documents, delivery only.
- A bill of exchange is an unconditional order in writing, addressed by one person to another, signed by the person giving it, requiring the person to whom it is addressed to pay on demand, or at a fixed or determinable future time, a sum certain in money to or to the order of a specified person, or to the bearer.
- A bill of exchange may be a specified payee bill or a bearer bill.

- The relevant parties to a bill of exchange are the drawer, drawee, payee, indorsee and holder.
- A holder of a bill may be a "holder for value" or a "holder in due course".

Essential Cases

Glasgow Pavilion Ltd v Motherwell (1903): a creditor is not required to receive payment of a debt due "by cheque or otherwise than in the current coin of the realm" and a creditor can even refuse Scottish bank notes.

Connal & Co v Loder (1868): in the case of transfer by negotiation, there is no requirement for (1) intimation of the transfer of the debt to the account debtor or (2) a separate document of transfer.

Hamilton v Spottiswoode (1849): the words "we hereby authorise you to pay" on a document were insufficient to constitute an "unconditional order".

Roffey v Greenwell (1839): a bill may provide for payment in the future provided that the future event is certain to happen, for example on the death of the drawer.

Clutton & Co v Attenborough & Son (1897): a bill will be valid where it is expressed to be payable to a person holding a particular office, or, if the specified person does not exist or is fictitious, the bill is treated as being payable to the bearer.

Hopkinson v Forster (1874): a drawee will only be liable on a bill when they accept liability on the bill; and, where they refuse to accept such liability, they may be liable directly to the drawer who drew up the bill.

British Linen Bank v Carruthers (1883): authority for the "funds attached" rule which applies to bills of exchange in terms of s 53(2) of the 1882 Act.

8 CONSUMER CREDIT

FORMS OF CONSUMER CREDIT

The Consumer Credit Act 1974 ("the Act") governs the regulation of various forms of credit made available to consumers. Credit may be provided in a number of guises.

Lender credit

The most straightforward kind of credit is lender credit. Here, a lender advances credit facilities to a customer in return for the customer repaying the credit over a definite or an indefinite period of time in standard payments, together with fixed or variable interest rates. Term loan facilities and overdraft facilities advanced by financial institutions, banks and building societies fall into this "lender credit" category. Lender credit may be secured over the assets of the customer (for example, a standard security) or it may be unsecured.

Vendor credit

The other kind of credit regulated by the Act is "vendor credit". Here, the vendor (seller) of goods extends credit to a buyer in relation to the sale of its goods to the buyer. The best-known form of "vendor credit" is hire-purchase. Here, the seller of goods transfers possession of the goods to the debtor – but title to the goods does not pass to the debtor. A hire-purchase contract is not a contract of sale and so the Sale of Goods Act 1979 does not apply to the former kind of contract (*Helby* v *Matthews* (1895)). A hire-purchase agreement is entered into between the seller and the debtor whereby the seller hires the goods to the debtor in return for the debtor making regular payments to the seller. At the end of the duration of the hire payments, the agreement confers an option – but not an obligation – in favour of the debtor to purchase the goods on the transfer of a final nominal payment to the seller. Hire-purchase can be contrasted with a contract of hire by virtue of the fact that in the latter there is no option or intention to transfer title to the goods to the buyer/debtor.

Credit sale and conditional sale agreements

Another form of vendor credit is the credit sale agreement. Here, title to the goods passes immediately from the seller to the buyer/debtor. The buyer/debtor then makes payments to the seller in instalments. This can be contrasted with a conditional sale agreement. This kind of contract is different since title only passes to the buyer on the payment of the final instalment. Conditional sale agreements resemble hire-purchase agreements. However, the distinguishing factor is that title passes to the buyer automatically on the payment of the final instalment in the case of a conditional sale agreement, whereas, in the case of hire-purchase, payment of the final instalment simply confers an option on the debtor to purchase the goods, that is, a sale is not certain. The crucial point is that hire-purchase does not necessarily involve a sale. However, credit sale and conditional sale agreements are, by definition, sales.

Credit cards

Credit cards are also regulated by the Act. The majority of credit cards permit customers to use the card up to a pre-arranged credit limit. When the customer presents their credit card to a seller/merchant, the seller/merchant is entitled to, and claims, payment from the credit card company. The customer is then liable to pay the credit card company the sum remitted to the seller/merchant pursuant to the sale transaction. The legal characteristics of a credit card arrangement were analysed in detail by the Court of Appeal in *Re Charge Card Services (No 2)* (1989). The court explained that a credit card transaction was made up of three separate contracts, as follows:

- a contract between the credit card company and the seller/merchant in terms of which the credit card company agrees to pay the seller/merchant in respect of the goods or services acquired by the customer and the seller/merchant agrees to accept payment from the credit card company;

- a contract between the credit card company and the customer in terms of which the customer is issued with a credit card which empowers them to purchase goods or services from sellers/merchants and the customer agrees to make payment for those goods or services to the credit card company together with interest; and

- a contract between the customer and the seller/merchant in terms of which (a) the latter agrees to sell goods or supply services to the former and (b) the latter agrees to accept payment for the goods or services via a credit card in substitution for payment by cash.

Thus, in a credit card arrangement, the seller/merchant agrees to accept the credit card company having an obligation to pay as opposed to the customer assuming an obligation to pay the seller/merchant directly. Hence, if the customer tenders payment by credit card, their liability to the seller/ merchant to make payment for the goods is immediately discharged.

REGULATED AGREEMENTS

The Act provides for the regulation of the provision of credit. The regulatory reach of the Act extends to consumer credit agreements and consumer hire agreements, other than exempt agreements outlined in the Financial Services and Markets Act 2000 (Regulated Activities) Order 2001 (SI 2001/544)), such as a credit agreement for more than £25,000 which is entered into by the borrower for business purposes. Agreements regulated by the Act are referred to generically as "regulated agreements". The Act deals with such agreements entered into by individuals and an "individual" is defined in s 189(1) of the Act. As well as an actual human being, it includes a partnership consisting of two or three persons not all of whom are bodies corporate and an unincorporated body of persons which does not consist entirely of bodies corporate and is not a partnership.

Consumer credit agreement

Section 8(1) of the Act provides that a consumer credit agreement is an agreement in terms of which the creditor gives the debtor credit of any amount. The definition of "credit" in s 9(1) of the Act is particularly wide, to the effect that it covers a cash loan or any other form of financial accommodation. Thus, it is sufficiently broad to include hire-purchase contracts, conditional sale contracts and credit sale contracts. In calculating the amount of credit, s 9(4) directs that the total charge for credit is excluded. The total charge for credit is defined by ss 20 and 189 of the Act and the Financial Services and Markets Act 2000 (Regulated Activities) Order 2001 (SI 2001/544).

Types of consumer credit agreement

Consumer credit agreements are classified based on their purposes rather than the legal forms which they take. The most significant are:

- *running-account credit* – in terms of s 10(1)(a) of the Act, such credit is of the type where the debtor has the right to obtain cash, goods or services from the creditor from time to time, to an amount or value whereby the credit limit (if any) is not exceeded (for example, a store card, credit card or overdraft);
- *fixed-sum credit* – under s 10(1)(b) of the Act this is any other facility under a consumer credit agreement whereby the debtor

receives credit in one amount or fixed instalments – in essence this is a form of credit where the sum does not vary (for example, a loan or hire-purchase agreement);

- *restricted-use credit* – s 11(1) of the Act provides that such credit is used to finance a specific transaction between the debtor and creditor or supplier (for example, a hire-purchase agreement);

- *unrestricted-use credit* – this enables the debtor to use credit as they wish in terms of s 11(2) of the Act (for example, an overdraft);

- *debtor–creditor agreements* – by virtue of s 13 of the Act, this is an agreement between a debtor and creditor for the extension of credit without the supplier of the goods or services being involved in the arrangement at all;

- *debtor–creditor–supplier agreements* – such contracts may involve two parties (for example, a debtor and supplier where the supplier sells goods and extends credit to the debtor to enable them to purchase the goods) or three parties, namely a debtor, creditor and supplier (for example, a credit card).

A consumer credit agreement must be either a debtor–creditor agreement or a debtor–creditor–supplier agreement.

Consumer hire agreement

Section 15 directs that a consumer hire agreement is an agreement to hire goods entered into by an individual which is not a hire-purchase agreement and is capable of lasting for more than 3 months in duration. With regard to the latter criterion, the fact that either party has a contractual right at any time to terminate an agreement of indefinite duration does not deprive that agreement of the status of a consumer hire agreement.

CONTROLS ON ENTERING INTO AGREEMENTS

Pre-contractual information and explanations

Section 55 of the Act and relevant statutory instruments (the Consumer Credit (Disclosure of Information) Regulations 2004 (SI 2004/1481) and the Consumer Credit (Disclosure of Information) Regulations 2010 (SI 2010/1013)) enjoin creditors or owners to provide certain information to the debtor or hirer before a consumer credit or consumer hire agreement is formed. In terms of s 55(2) of the Act, the effect of a failure to perform such obligations means that a court order is required before the creditor can enforce the agreement against the debtor or hirer. Section 55C further provides that the debtor must be provided with a copy of the prospective agreement without delay. There are additional requirements contained in the Financial Conduct Authority's *Consumer Credit Sourcebook* at r 4.2.5 and r 5.2A.

A further consideration is s 56 which regulates antecedent negotiations, that is, any negotiations entered into between the debtor or hirer and (i) the creditor or owner, (ii) a credit broker who supplies the creditor with goods to be supplied to the debtor under a debtor–creditor–supplier agreement or (iii) the supplier in a debtor–creditor–supplier agreement. Section 56(4) states that negotiations commence when the debtor and the negotiator begin communications (including by advertisement), and incorporating all dealings, dialogue or representations made by the negotiator to the debtor. Under s 56(3) of the Act an agreement is void insofar as it attempts to negate the creditor's liability for the acts or omissions of the negotiator or make the negotiator the debtor's agent.

Control of content and form

Section 60 of the Act goes on to control the content and form of consumer credit and consumer hire agreements. Certain prescribed information must be contained in the agreements and such information must be given prominence, be distinguishable and easily legible. Moreover, information of a financial nature must be presented as a whole. The requisite content is governed by the Consumer Credit (Agreements) Regulations 1983 (SI 1983/1553) or the Consumer Credit (Agreements) Regulations 2010 (SI 2010/1014) (depending on the exact nature of the regulated agreement, with the latter regime applying, for example, to most instances of personal unsecured credit) and includes the following:

- the names and addresses of the parties;
- a prominent heading on the first page detailing the legal nature of the agreement, for example that it is a hire-purchase agreement regulated under the Act;
- the cash price (where appropriate).

Section 61 provides for the execution of regulated agreements. Section 61(1) of the Act directs that the creditor or owner and the debtor or hirer must sign the agreement in proper form in the signature box, that the agreement must embody all the terms (except those implied by law) and that it is legible. A further requirement for proper execution is the provision of a copy of the executed agreement to the debtor, in terms of s 61A, unless the agreement is an excluded agreement (as defined in that section). All of the above prescribed content must be included in the agreement. If it is not so included, the effect is that the Act will have been breached. If the agreement is not properly executed, the effect of s 65(1) and (2) of the Act is that it cannot be enforced against the debtor or hirer (in terms of retaking possession of the goods) without the leave of the court. If the agreement may be cancelled in terms of the Act, it must contain the information prescribed in s 64 of the Act concerning the cancellation rights and their exercise.

Delivery of copies of executed and unexecuted agreements

All copies of the agreement require to be supplied to the debtor or hirer by the creditor, owner or negotiator.

Sections 62 and 63 of the Act deal with the delivery of copies of unexecuted and executed agreements to the debtor or hirer. In circumstances where the creditor or owner has signed the agreement before the debtor or hirer signs it, s 63(1) of the Act stipulates that a copy of the executed agreement, and of any other document referred to in it, must be there and then delivered to the debtor or hirer. However, if the agreement has not been signed by the creditor or owner when it is presented to the debtor or hirer for signature, then the debtor or hirer must be given a copy of the agreement on signing it together with a further copy of the executed agreement, and of any other document referred to in it, within 7 days of the creditor or owner signing it. Where an overdraft is involved, s 61B requires the terms of the agreement to be set out in a document and given to the debtor.

Right to withdraw

The Act provides the debtor or hirer with certain rights to withdraw from a consumer credit or consumer hire agreement. If the creditor or owner has not signed the agreement at the point in time when the debtor or hirer signs it, the debtor or hirer is entitled to withdraw from the prospective agreement at any time before the former signs. Section 57(2) and (3) of the Act regulates the manner of withdrawal to the effect that written or oral notice of withdrawal may be given by the creditor or owner and others. In terms of s 57(1) of the Act, the effect of a withdrawal is the same as a cancellation of the regulated agreement under s 69 of the Act.

Right of withdrawal or cancellation

The withdrawal or cancellation of regulated agreements is governed by s 66A or, where that section does not apply, s 67 of the Act. The right of withdrawal is the stronger of the two, from the perspective of the debtor. It allows the debtor in some regulated consumer credit agreements to withdraw without giving any reason. The debtor has 14 days from the day after the date of the agreement, or a later date where there has been some delay in finalising details, to give oral or written notice of withdrawal. An agreement is excluded from this right of withdrawal where it is:

- an agreement for credit exceeding £60,260;
- an agreement secured on land;
- a restricted-use credit agreement to finance the purchase of land; or
- an agreement for a bridging loan in connection with the purchase of land.

Section 67 applies where section 66A does not and entitles the debtor to cancel where oral representations are made by an individual acting as a negotiator (see above for a definition of who may constitute a negotiator) or someone on their behalf in the presence of the debtor or hirer in the course of antecedent negotiations where the agreement was signed by the debtor or hirer away from trade premises of the creditor, owner or negotiator. In these circumstances, the debtor is given a period of time in which to reflect on whether they wish to proceed with the agreement or to cancel it. A representation is any statement of fact or opinion made before the contract is executed which is material to any of the matters being negotiated and capable of influencing the debtor's or hirer's judgement of whether or not to enter into the agreement or which is capable of inducing the debtor or hirer to enter into the agreement, whether or not the negotiator intended such statement to induce entry into the agreement (*Moorgate Services* v *Kabir* (1995)).

As noted above, s 64 directs that details of cancellation rights must be provided. Section 64(1) of the Act directs that in circumstances where an agreement is a cancellable agreement (defined as an agreement that can be cancelled under s 67), every copy of the agreement must include a notice in the prescribed form indicating the right of the debtor or hirer to cancel, how and when that right may be exercised and to whom (including the address) that notice of cancellation may be sent.

The point in time at which the notice referred to above in terms of s 64(1)(b) of the Act or the second copy of the agreement is sent dictates when the cooling-off period of 5 days referred to in s 68 of the Act ends. The effect of ss 68(1) and 69(1) of the Act is that a debtor or hirer may cancel a regulated agreement within the cooling-off period, which begins when the debtor or hirer signs the agreement and continues until 5 days after the date when the debtor or hirer receives the s 64(1)(b) notice or the second copy of the agreement. The notice must be in writing and must be sent to the creditor or owner or their agent or to someone specified in the s 64(1)(b) notice. It does not require to be in any particular form. However, it must indicate the intention of the debtor or hirer to withdraw from the agreement.

Consequences of cancellation

Section 69(1) of the Act stipulates that the service of a notice of cancellation operates to cancel the agreement. Section 70(1) of the Act provides that any sums paid under the agreement are repayable by the creditor or owner to the debtor or hirer. Sums which are stated to be payable by the debtor or hirer under the agreement cease to be so payable but sums paid by the creditor or owner to a supplier on behalf of the debtor or hirer under a debtor–creditor–supplier agreement become repayable to the creditor. The effect of s 72(4) of the Act is that (subject to any lien) goods held by the debtor or hirer must be returned to the creditor or owner. Where s 66A applies, there are similar provisions for restoring the *status quo ante*.

MATTERS ARISING DURING THE CURRENCY OF THE AGREEMENT

Provision of information

Sections 77, 77A, 77B, 78, 78A, 79 and 80 of the Act provide for the provision of information on request and statements automatically to the debtor or hirer in the case of a fixed-sum credit agreement, running-account credit agreement or consumer hire agreement. On request, during the course of a regulated agreement, a debtor or hirer may obtain a copy of the agreement and a statement of the account between them from the creditor. Sections 77, 78 and 79 of the Act direct that the statement in the case of a fixed-sum creditor agreement, running-account credit agreement and/or a consumer hire agreement must include a note of the sums paid to date by the debtor, sums remaining unpaid and the remaining total sums to be paid. If the creditor fails to respond in compliance with these rules, they will not be entitled to enforce the agreement so long as they continue to remain in default. Section 78A also deals with the provision of information about interest rate changes to certain consumer credit agreements, with such a change not permissible unless the debtor has been informed in writing.

Implied terms

A consumer credit or consumer hire agreement will consist of particular express and implied terms. The implied terms included within various types of contract, such as sales contracts, hire-purchase agreements and hire agreements are statutory in origin and are now found in the Consumer Rights Act 2015 (the "2015 Act"). For example, s 9 of the 2015 Act provides that goods must be of satisfactory quality and reasonably fit for purpose and s 10 specifies that goods must be fit for any particular purpose the consumer makes known to the trader before the contract is made. Under s 11 of the 2015 Act there is an implied term that goods will correspond to their description. Section 13 provides that goods must conform to sample and s 14 states that they should match a model seen or examined. In s 17 of the 2015 Act there is an implied term on the part of the creditor that they will have a right to transfer possession or sell or transfer the goods (as appropriate) at the relevant time, that the goods are free and will remain free from any charges or encumbrances until ownership of the goods is to pass and that the consumer will enjoy quiet possession of the goods. For cases falling outside the provisions of the 2015 Act (ie not involving a trader supplying goods to a consumer), ss 8–11 of the Supply of Goods (Implied Terms) Act 1973 contain implied terms for hire-purchases that are similar to those contained in the 2015 Act and mirror those in ss 12–15 of the Sale of Goods Act 1979. Likewise, ss 7–10 of the Supply of Goods and Services Act 1982 provide that similar implied terms apply in the case of contracts of hire that lie beyond the scope of the 2015 Act.

Section 75: connected lender liability

The concept of connected lender liability is found in s 75 of the Act and implicit within it is a recognition that trade sellers and finance companies usually have a close relationship. The basic premise of s 75 of the Act is that breaches of a contract of sale by a trade seller will have implications for the creditor in terms of the back-to-back consumer credit or consumer hire agreement. It directs that if a debtor under a debtor–creditor–supplier agreement involving three parties has, in relation to a transaction financed by the agreement, any claim against the supplier in respect of a misrepresentation or breach of contract, they shall have a like claim against the creditor, who will be jointly and severally liable to the debtor alongside the supplier. So if the supplier is liable to the debtor for breach of contract or misrepresentation, the creditor will also be liable. This provision is particularly useful for, and protective of, consumers in a credit card transaction.

In the case of *OFT* v *Lloyds TSB Bank plc* (2007), the Court of Appeal held that s 75 also applies to credit card transactions involving a fourth-party merchant acquirer. Moreover, the House of Lords in the same case confirmed that s 75 also applied to purchases made abroad by debtors with a credit card. However, s 187(3A) of the Act specifically directs that s 75 of the Act does not apply to debit cards.

There has been some uncertainty over the years as to the effect of s 75 on the credit agreement where there has been a breach of the supply contract and whether it enables a debtor to rescind both. It was held by the UK Supreme Court in *Durkin* v *DSG Retail Ltd* (2014) that the law implies a term into a credit agreement that it is conditional upon the survival of the supply agreement, and the rejection of goods and rescinding of the supply agreement by the debtor for breach of contract enables them to use the implied term to rescind the credit agreement.

TERMINATION AND DEFAULT OF REGULATED AGREEMENTS

Section 94 of the Act stipulates that a debtor is entitled at any time to terminate a regulated agreement by providing notice to the creditor and making payment to the creditor of all amounts due. The notice may embody the exercise by the debtor of any option to purchase goods conferred on them by the agreement, and deal with any other matter arising on, or in relation to, the termination of the agreement. Section 95 of the Act states that the debtor will have the right to a rebate on the charge for credit which is calculated in accordance with the rules set out in the Consumer Credit (Early Settlement) Regulations 2004 (SI 2004/1483). Since the Consumer Credit (EU Directive) Regulations 2010 (SI 2010/1010), there is also provision to make partial discharge of a consumer credit agreement (not secured on land) under s 94(3), with the aforementioned 2004 Regulations providing a calculation for that process.

Termination of hire-purchase and conditional sale agreements by debtor or hirer

Section 99(1) of the Act provides that a debtor or hirer under a hire-purchase agreement or conditional sale agreement is entitled to terminate it and return the goods at any time before the final payment falls due in terms of the agreement by providing notice to persons authorised to receive payments in terms of the agreement. By virtue of s 99(2) of the Act, the termination of such an agreement does not affect any liability under the agreement which has accrued before the termination: that is, the debtor or hirer is not relieved of any liability for payments due before termination.

However, s 100(1) of the Act directs that the debtor must pay the creditor up to half the total price in terms of the agreement if the debtor takes advantage of the s 99 right to terminate early. If the court is satisfied that a sum less than that amount would be equal to the loss sustained by the creditor in consequence of the termination of the agreement by the debtor, the court may make an order for the payment of that sum in lieu of that amount. Thus, on the face of it, ss 99 and 100 are useful for a debtor who is struggling to make payments in terms of the regulated agreement. Nevertheless, in practice, regulated agreements will commonly contain an accelerated payments clause which stipulates that the debtor is obliged to make all payments under the agreement in the event that the debtor defaults on any payment: that is, all payments become due and payable. In the case of *Wadham Stringer Finance Ltd* v *Meaney* (1981), it was held that such an accelerated payments clause will not be a common-law penalty where the creditor affords the debtor a rebate for early settlement. However, ss 62 and 63 of, and Sch 2 to, the Consumer Rights Act 2015 may have rendered at least some such clauses ineffective as unfair terms. In any event, in terms of s 87(1) of the Act, the creditor must serve a default notice on the debtor before such an accelerated payments clause can have immediate effect.

Creditor's right to repossess goods in the case of hire-purchase and conditional sale agreements

In circumstances where the debtor defaults without seeking to terminate a hire-purchase or conditional sale agreement, the creditor may look to repossess the goods hired. In terms of s 90(1) of the Act, where the debtor has paid a reasonable number of instalments for the goods, namely one-third of the total price or more, the creditor must first obtain an order from the court to repossess the goods "from the debtor". Section 90(7) of the Act refers to the goods as "protected goods". The consequences of a breach of s 90 by the creditor are outlined in s 91 of the Act to the effect that the agreement, if not previously terminated, shall terminate and the debtor is released from all liability under the agreement and has the right to recover all sums already paid. However, the creditor may retake possession of the goods without breaching s 90 if:

- the debtor has transferred the goods to a third party (consider *Bentinck* v *Cromwell Engineering Ltd* (1971) where a car was left in a garage);
- the debtor has abandoned the goods; or
- the debtor permits the creditor to repossess the goods (see *Mercantile Credit Co* v *Cross* (1965)).

Termination of consumer hire agreements by hirer

Section 101(1) and (3) of the Act deal specifically with consumer hire agreements. Notwithstanding the fact that a consumer hire agreement may be of an indefinite duration, it is provided that the hirer is entitled to terminate the agreement by giving notice to the owner or any person entitled or authorised to receive the sums payable under the agreement where that agreement has endured for a period of at least 18 months. In terms of s 101(4) and (5) of the Act, the period in respect of which the hirer is obliged to give notice to the creditor represents the shorter of 3 months and the period between hire payments. However, there are certain circumstances where termination of a consumer hire agreement is excluded in terms of s 101(7) of the Act as follows:

• where the agreement provides for payment which in total exceeds £1,500 per annum;
• where the goods are hired by the hirer for business purposes and the goods are selected by the hirer, which are then acquired by the owner from a third party at his request; or
• where, in terms of the agreement, the hirer requires the goods for the purposes of hiring them to third parties in the course of a business.

Provision of information to debtors and hirers

Debtors who are struggling to meet their payments under a regulated agreement are entitled to various items of information. First, by virtue of s 86B of the Act, the creditor must serve a notice of arrears upon the debtor in prescribed form (in terms of the Consumer Credit (Information Requirements and Duration of Licences and Charges) Regulations 2007 (SI 2007/1167)) in circumstances where the debtor has entered into a consumer hire agreement or fixed-sum agreement and has fallen two payments behind. That notice must be served within 14 days of the debtor falling two payments behind.

Second, the provisions of ss 86E and 187A of the Act stipulate that the creditor must serve a default sum notice on the debtor where the debtor is due to pay a default sum under the agreement as a result of a breach of the agreement. The notice of such default sums must be served within the prescribed period after the default sum becomes payable according to s 86E(2) of the Act. In accordance with s 86E(5) of the Act, if the creditor or owner fails to serve the default sum notice upon the debtor or hirer within the prescribed period mentioned, they shall not be entitled to enforce the agreement until the notice is given to the debtor or hirer.

Third, according to s 86A of the Act, the Financial Conduct Authority is entrusted with the preparation of an arrears information sheet and a default information sheet. The purpose of these information sheets is to provide debtors and hirers with assistance so that they are aware of the effects of notices of arrears and/or default sum notices which may have been served upon them by the creditor or owner in terms of ss 86B and/ or 86C (which relates to running-account credits) of the Act. The creditor and owner are under a duty to send such sheets to debtors or hirers when they send notices of arrears or default sum notices.

Default notices

Where the debtor is in breach of a regulated agreement, the creditor or owner must first serve a default notice upon the debtor or hirer before they may enforce their rights under the agreement. Section 87(1) of the Act states that the creditor is prevented from exercising each of the following enforcement remedies listed in s 87 unless they have first served such a default notice in the prescribed form (in terms of the Consumer Credit (Enforcement, Default and Termination Notices) Regulations 1983 (SI 1983/1561)) upon the debtor:

- the right to terminate the agreement;
- the right to demand early payment of any sum, for example in terms of a contractually agreed accelerated payments clause;
- the right to recover possession of the goods sold or hired;
- the treatment of any of the debtor's rights as terminated, deferred or restricted; or
- the right to enforce any security.

There is no requirement for a creditor to serve a default notice upon a debtor in order to sue for sums which are already due and payable under the agreement.

Content and form of default notices

The content of the notice is governed by s 88 as follows:

- it must contain details of the breach;
- it must outline what must be done in order to remedy the breach, in the event that it is remediable, and when this must be done;

- it must set out what sum is required to be paid as compensation for the breach in the case of an irremediable breach, together with a notice of the date before which it is to be paid; and

- it must contain a statement regarding the implications of a failure on the part of the debtor to remedy the defect or pay the sum.

The period permitted for payment must be at least 14 days from the date of the service of the notice upon the debtor. A default notice will be invalid where the sum due is overstated in the default notice (*Woodchester Lease Management Services Ltd* v *Swain* (1999)).

Where the debtor complies with the default notice, for example by making payment within the stipulated 14 days, s 89 of the Act states that the breach will be treated as if it had never occurred. However, a failure on the part of the debtor to take the requisite action in terms of the default notice within the 14-day period entitles the creditor to take the enforcement remedies under s 87 of the Act (see above). Finally, in terms of ss 76 and 98 of the Act, the creditor must give the debtor a separate notice called a non-default notice before it exercises a right to do any of the following in circumstances where (1) that right is given to the creditor in terms of the agreement and (2) the debtor is not in breach of the agreement:

- the right to demand the early payment of any sum, for example in terms of a contractually agreed accelerated payments clause;
- the right to terminate the agreement; or
- the right to recover possession of the goods sold or hired.

This provision is applicable in situations where a clause of the agreement enables the creditor to do any of the above on the occurrence of a certain event which in itself does not amount to a breach of contract (for example, the insolvency of the debtor).

JUDICIAL CONTROL

The Act sets out a range of orders which may be granted by the court in relation to the control of consumer credit and consumer hire agreements. In prescribing such orders, the court also has a range of powers. For example, in terms of s 135 of the Act, the court has the power to make one of its orders duly conditional on the doing of some act or acts by any party to the proceedings. By virtue of s 136 of the Act, the court may, in any order made by it, include such provision as it considers just for amending any agreement or security in consequence of a term of the order.

The range of court orders

Where an agreement has been improperly executed, the terms of s 127 of the Act are such that a creditor must first obtain an enforcement order in advance of enforcing the agreement. Alternatively, the court may grant a time order. The objective of a time order (set out in s 129 of the Act) is to give the debtor extra time to pay. Such time orders may be sought by a debtor. Section 131 of the Act stipulates that a protection order is available on the application of a creditor or an owner. It protects the property of the creditor or owner from damage or depreciation pending the outcome of any proceedings which have been initiated under the Act. The court may also grant a return or transfer order in terms of s 133 of the Act where the agreement is a hire-purchase agreement or conditional sale agreement. In terms of a return order, the creditor is entitled to the return of the goods, whereas a transfer order involves a transfer of title of certain goods to the debtor with the remainder of the goods being returned to the creditor. Furthermore, where the court forms the view that the relationship established between the debtor and creditor in terms of a credit agreement is unfair to the debtor under s 140A (and see eg *Plevin* v *Paragon Personal Finance Limited* (2014)), the court has the power to make a number of orders in terms of s 140B of the Act. Such orders are of the nature that the court has a wide power to revise a credit agreement if it is minded to do so. Finally, the court may make an order under s 132 of the Act which provides financial relief to hirers in circumstances where the owner of the goods recovers them by virtue of, or without, taking court action.

Essential Facts

- The Consumer Credit Act 1974 ("the Act") regulates lender credit, vendor credit, credit sale agreements, conditional sale agreements and credit cards.
- Consumer credit agreements and consumer hire agreements are regulated by the Act.
- Pre-contractual information and the form and content of consumer credit agreements and consumer hire agreements are controlled by the Act.

- The Act provides a debtor with a right to withdraw and cancel a regulated agreement.
- Section 75 of the Act provides for connected lender liability whereby breaches of a contract of sale by a trade seller will have implications for the creditor in terms of the back-to-back consumer credit or consumer hire agreement.
- The Act regulates the termination of consumer hire agreements by the hirer and the termination of hire-purchase and conditional sale agreements by the debtor or hirer.
- Where the debtor is in breach of a regulated agreement, the creditor or owner must first serve a default notice upon the debtor or hirer before they may enforce their rights under the agreement.
- The courts are provided with the right to make a range of orders which control the content and exercise of rights of creditors under regulated agreements.

Essential Cases

Helby v Matthews (1895): a hire-purchase contract is not a contract of sale and so the Sale of Goods Act 1979 does not apply to the former kind of contract.

Re Charge Card Services (No 2) (1989): a credit card transaction comprises three separate contracts.

Moorgate Services v Kabir (1995): a representation is a statement of fact or opinion made before the contract is executed which is material to any of the matters being negotiated and capable of inducing the debtor or hirer to enter into the agreement or influencing the debtor's or hirer's judgement of whether or not to enter into the agreement.

OFT v Lloyds TSB Bank plc (2007): the Court of Appeal held that s 75 of the Act applied to credit card transactions involving a fourth-party merchant acquirer.

OFT v Lloyds TSB Bank plc (2007): the House of Lords confirmed that s 75 of the Act also applied to credit card purchases made abroad by debtors.

Durkin v DSG Retail Ltd (2014): there is an implied term in a credit agreement that it is conditional upon the survival of the supply agreement, and the rejection of goods and rescinding of the supply agreement by the debtor for breach of contract enables them to rescind the credit agreement.

Wadham Stringer Finance Ltd v Meaney (1981): an accelerated payments clause will not be a common-law penalty where the creditor affords the debtor a rebate for early settlement.

9 INTELLECTUAL PROPERTY

Many businesses own valuable assets which are intangible and represent the culmination of years of research and development. For example, a company may create a new method of doing something such as an invention or create a logo which differentiates that company or that company's products from its competitors. The company might be in the business of entertainment whereupon its songs, plays or written works attract great popular appeal. In such circumstances, the area of commercial law known as intellectual property assumes great importance. Intellectual property law establishes rules and procedures whereby such innovations or productions may be created, legally recognised and protected. In this chapter, we will consider the main types of intellectual property right which are recognised by the law, namely copyright, patents, trade marks and designs.

COPYRIGHT

Introduction

The law of copyright is governed by the Copyright, Designs and Patents Act 1988 ("CDPA"). In terms of ss 1–8 of CDPA, copyright may exist in literary, dramatic, musical or artistic works, films, broadcasts, sound recordings and typographical arrangements of published works. It is provided in s 3(1) of CDPA that a table or compilation, a computer program, the preparatory design material for a computer program and a database are all examples of a literary work. Dramatic works include works of dance or mime and a musical work means a work consisting of music, exclusive of any words or action intended to be sung, spoken or performed with the music.

Originality

There is a requirement that the literary, dramatic, musical or artistic work be "original" and "recorded, in writing or otherwise" in terms of ss 1(1)(a) and s 3(2) of CDPA. The threshold for demonstrating originality is not particularly onerous. The *dictum* of Peterson J in the case of *University of London Press Ltd* v *University Tutorial Press Ltd* (1916) is to the effect that the work does not require to be representative of the expression of original or inventive thought. It is enough that the originality relates to the expression of some thought. That requirement will be satisfied if the work has not been copied from another work and so has originated from the author. In *University of London Press*, it was held that exam papers would attract copyright protection.

The requirement for originality is complemented by the need for some expenditure of effort, skill and labour by the author in the case of a compilation work, that is, a work which adapts, organises or arranges an existing work or works. Moreover, the effect of the rule that the work must be recorded is that the law does not recognise copyright in ideas, only ideas which have been expressed or articulated. Sections 153–155 of CDPA also stipulate that there must be a sufficiently close connection between the UK and the author of the work, the place where it was first published or the place from which it was first made (if the work is one of broadcast) to attract copyright.

Authorship

Section 9 of CDPA defines the author as the person who creates the work, or the producer in the case of a sound recording, the producer and director in the case of a film, the person making the broadcast in the case of a broadcast, and the publisher in the case of the typographical arrangement of a published edition. The effect of being an author is delimited in s 11(1) of CDPA to the effect that the author is deemed to be the first owner of any copyright in it. However, there are exceptions: for example, where an employee makes the work *in the course of his employment*, his employer is the first owner of any copyright in the work subject to any agreement to the contrary. In the case of a literary, dramatic, musical or artistic work, the copyright endures for 70 years from the end of the calendar year in which the author dies, whereupon it expires, by virtue of s 12(2) of CDPA. A distinction should be made between the author and the owner and it ought to be emphasised that the author is relevant for the purposes of the 70-year rule, even in circumstances where the ownership of the copyright has been transferred. In the case of a film, s 13B(2) of CDPA directs that the copyright expires at the end of the period of 70 years from the end of the calendar year in which the death occurs of the last to die of the principal director, the author of the screenplay, the author of the dialogue, or the composer of music specially created for and used in the film. Sound recordings are provided for by s 13A(2) of CDPA, with copyright in the sound recording expiring at the end of the period of 50 years from the end of the calendar year in which the recording is made, or, if during that period the recording is published, 70 years from the end of the calendar year in which it is first published, or, if during that period the recording is not published but is released to the public by being played in public or communicated to the public, 70 years from the end of the calendar year in which it is first so made available.

The two components of copyright

The right of copyright consists of two components. First, there is the economic right which attaches to the copyright work. This enables the owner to exploit the work for financial reward, for example by being paid every time that the work is published, played, transmitted, shown, etc. It also confers upon the owner the right to prevent unlicensed reproduction and dealings in the work. It is the economic right that is essentially a property right: that is, since the owner owns the copyright, he may alienate it, license it, grant security over it, in return for a loan, etc. Note that copyright arises automatically by operation of law. There is no requirement for registration in order to constitute copyright. It is also possible for copyright to be owned jointly by more than one person. Copyright can be contrasted with moral rights. Moral rights recognise interests of the author other than economic rights, and are continuing in nature.

Moral rights

An author will have moral rights even in circumstances where they have assigned their ownership of the copyright or the physical form of the work first recorded. First, where the author has asserted their moral rights in accordance with s 78 of CDPA, s 77 provides that the author has the right of paternity, that is, the right to be identified as the author of the literary, dramatic, musical or artistic work or as the director of the film. The second moral right is the right of integrity, which entitles the author or director to prevent their work from being treated in a derogatory fashion in terms of s 80(1) of CDPA. The provisions of s 80(2)(b) of CDPA state that the author's or director's work is treated in a derogatory manner if it is distorted or mutilated or is otherwise treated in a manner which is prejudicial to the honour or reputation of the author or director. Section 84 of CDPA also provides the author with the right not to have a literary, dramatic, musical or artistic work falsely attributed to them as author or director. Section 85 of CDPA also provides that a person who for private and domestic purposes commissions the taking of a photograph or the making of a film has a right of privacy in respect of such works, where copyright subsists in the resulting works. However, the right of privacy does not confer a separate right of ownership in copyright in favour of that person who commissioned the work. Finally, in terms of reg 3 of the Artist's Resale Right Regulations 2006 (SI 2006/346), the creators of works of graphic or plastic art such as a picture, a collage, a painting, a drawing, an engraving, a print, a lithograph, a sculpture, a tapestry, a ceramic, an item of glassware or a photograph, enjoy a right ("resale right") to a royalty on any sale of the work which is a resale subsequent to the first transfer of ownership by the author.

It is not possible to alienate a moral right except where the person entitled to the moral right is deceased. Moral rights, with the exception of the resale right under reg 3 of the Artist's Resale Right Regulations 2006, may be waived. All moral rights endure for the same period as the economic rights, except for the false attribution right under s 84 of CDPA, which endures for 20 years after the death of the author or director (in terms of s 86 of CDPA). The holder of a moral right has the right to be protected against any infringement which is to be treated as a breach of a statutory duty in terms of s 103(1) of CDPA. However, whether this means that remedies other than the usual remedies are available on a civil action is unclear.

Protection from primary and secondary infringement

The copyright owner has the benefit of two forms of protection, namely the right to be protected in respect of primary infringement and secondary infringement. With regard to primary infringement, in terms of s 16 of CDPA, the copyright owner has the exclusive right to do certain acts in relation to the works in the UK, namely:

- to copy the work;
- to issue copies of the work to the public;
- to rent or lend the work to the public;
- to perform, show or play the work in public;
- to communicate the work to the public; or
- to make an adaptation of the work or do any of the other restricted acts in relation to an adaptation.

In the event that the above acts are performed by a third party without the consent of the copyright owner, the right has been infringed. CDPA then goes on to regulate secondary infringement, being when a third party deals in infringing copies of copyright works without the licence of the copyright owner. Secondary infringement involves the situation where the third party provides the means for making infringing copies (s 24), permitting the use of premises for infringing performances (s 25) and the provision of apparatus for infringing performances (s 26). "Infringing copy" is defined in s 27, namely that an article whose very creation constituted an infringement of the copyright in the work in question is an infringing copy.

Non-infringement

The coverage of the protection enjoyed by the copyright owner is limited to the right to prevent the copying of the work. Thus, it stands to reason that copyright does not enable the copyright owner to take action against a person who independently creates the same work, for example inadvertently. It should also be noted that there are certain exceptions for legitimate use of copyrighted works, such as research and private study where that is accompanied with sufficient acknowledgement (s 29).

Orphan works

Section 116A of CDPA, introduced by the Enterprise and Regulatory Reform Act 2013, made provision in relation to the licensing of "orphan works" – that is, works with no identifiable author – for use. The key test for allowing the use of creative work without an owner's explicit permission is that a "diligent search" for the owner of the copyright has taken place.

PATENTS

Introduction

The regulation of patents is governed by CDPA, the Patents Act 1977 (the "1977 Act") and the Patents Act 2004 (the "2004 Act"). A patent right may be granted in respect of an invention. Section 1(1) of the 1977 Act stipulates that a patent may be granted only for an invention in respect of which certain conditions are satisfied, namely that the invention is new, involves an inventive step and is capable of industrial application. Further, by virtue of s 1(3) of the 1977 Act, it is provided that a patent must not be granted for an invention the commercial exploitation of which would be contrary to public policy or morality.

"New", "inventive step"

Section 2(1) of the 1977 Act states that an invention will be taken to be new if it does not form part of the state of the art at the priority date (which is stipulated as commonly being the date of filing of the application for registration of the patent in terms of s 5 of the 1977 Act), the state of the art comprising all matter by written or oral description by use or in any other way (see *Arrow Generics Ltd* v *Akzo NV* (2008)). With regard to what is meant by an "inventive step", the relevant provision is s 3 of the 1977 Act, which directs that an inventive step will be one which is not obvious to a person skilled in the art, having regard to any matter which forms part of the state of the art: that is, it must introduce a new idea to the state of knowledge existing at the time (*Pozzoli SpA* v *BDMO SA* (2007)). Section 4 directs that the requirement that the inventive step be capable of industrial application means that it must be capable of being made or used in any kind of industry, including agriculture, that is to say that it performs a useful technical purpose.

Exceptions

In terms of ss 1(2) and 4A(1) of the 1977 Act, certain things are deemed not to be patentable inventions: first, anything which consists of a discovery, scientific theory or mathematical method; second, a method of treatment of the human or animal body by surgery or therapy, or a method of diagnosis practised on the human or animal body; third, a literary, dramatic, musical or artistic work or any other aesthetic creation; fourth, a scheme, rule or method for performing a mental act; fifth, playing a game or doing business; and, finally, a program for a computer and the presentation of information.

Registration

It will commonly be the person who has created the invention who will become the registered owner of a patent. However, this is not always the case. For example, in terms of s 39 of the 1977 Act, an employer will be deemed to own an invention and have the right to register it as a patent where it is created by their employee, *inter alia*, in the course of the employee's normal duties and an invention might reasonably be expected to result from the carrying out of those duties. In order to be patented, an invention must be registered with the UK Intellectual Property Office ("UKIPO") in respect of a UK patent or the European Patent Office for a patent in respect of certain identified European countries. An application for a patent is made in accordance with s 14 of the 1977 Act. Section 14 provides that every application for a patent must be set out in the prescribed form and filed at the UKIPO duly containing a request for the grant of a patent, a specification containing a description of the invention, a claim or claims defining the extent of the monopoly sought by the inventor and any drawing referred to in the description or any claim together with an abstract. Section 14(3) of the 1977 Act stipulates that the specification must disclose the invention in a manner which is clear enough and complete enough for the invention to be reproduced by a person skilled in the art. The claim or claims within the specification must define the matter for which the applicant seeks protection, be clear and concise, be supported by the description and relate to one invention or to a group of inventions which are so linked as to form a single inventive concept.

Pre-registration screening

When the UKIPO receives the application, it is subjected to a process of preliminary examination by an examiner in order to determine whether the requirements of the 1977 Act have been satisfied all in accordance with s 15A of the 1977 Act. The terms of s 16 of the 1977 Act provide for subsequent publication of the application as it was filed. A substantive examination and search of the application is then made in accordance with ss 17 and 18 of the 1977 Act and the examiner will then decide whether to grant and publish the application in its final form. In terms of s 24 of the 1977 Act, as soon as practicable after a patent has been granted, a notice that the patent has been granted must be published and a certificate in the prescribed form must be sent to the proprietor of the patent that the patent has been granted to the proprietor. Once granted, by virtue of s 25 of the 1977 Act, a patent will take effect from the date of filing of the application for a period of up to 20 years.

Nature of right

Section 31(2) of the 1977 Act directs that a patent right is a form of incorporeal moveable property in terms of Scots law. The owner of the patent has the right to sell it or license it to third parties in return for the payment of royalties, etc. The patent right confers a right in favour of the patent owner to prevent third parties from using the invention for a period of up to 20 years in the UK, that is, an exclusionary right. The patent does not always confer a positive right to exploit the invention: for example, where the patent improves upon an invention which was already patented.

Protection from infringement

Section 60(1) of the 1977 Act governs the circumstances in which a third party will be deemed to have infringed a patent owner's patent. First, a third party infringes a patent over a product where he makes, disposes of, offers to dispose of, uses or imports that product or keeps it whether for disposal or otherwise in the UK without the consent of the owner of the patent. Second, a third party infringes a patent in respect of a process where he uses the process or offers it for use in the United Kingdom when he knows, or it is obvious to a reasonable person in the circumstances, that its use there without the consent of the proprietor would be an infringement of the patent. Third, a third party will be deemed to have infringed a patent for a process where he disposes of, offers to dispose of, uses or imports any product obtained directly by means of that process or keeps any such product whether for disposal or otherwise in the UK without the consent of the owner of the patent. Finally, a third party also infringes a patent for an invention if, while the patent is in force and without the consent of the proprietor, he supplies or offers to supply in the UK a person (other than a licensee or other person entitled to work the invention) with any of the means, relating to an essential element of the invention, for putting the invention into effect when he knows, or it is obvious to a reasonable person in the circumstances, that those means are suitable for putting, and are intended to put, the invention into effect in the UK.

Exceptions

However, there are exceptions to infringement set out in s 60(5) of the 1977 Act, which provides that a third party will not be guilty of infringement in circumstances where the use of the patent is done by the third party privately and for non-commercial purposes or for experimental purposes relating to the subject-matter of the invention, among other matters. In order to prove infringement, the specification and claim of the patent owner is compared against the product or process of the defender. Whether the product or process of the third party amounts to an infringement is essentially a factual test, but it need not be identical in order to amount to an infringement. The case of *Gormully and Jeffery Manufacturing Co v North British Rubber Co Ltd* (1898) demonstrates that the courts will apply the "pith and marrow" doctrine to the effect that the court will separate the essential features of the specification from the inessential features. Where the essential aspects of the specification are copied, then infringement is established even though the final product differs as regards the features of the specification which are inessential.

TRADE MARKS

Introduction

Section 1(1) of the Trade Marks Act 1994 (the "1994 Act") directs that a trade mark is any sign capable of being represented graphically which is capable of distinguishing goods or services of one undertaking from those of other undertakings. Once registered with the UKIPO, the trade mark represents a property right which is vested in the proprietor and the proprietor is entitled to various protections, namely the right and remedies contained in the 1994 Act, and in particular the exclusive rights conferred by s 9 of the 1994 Act. In terms of s 22 of the 1994 Act, a registered trade mark is a form of incorporeal moveable property. Without registration, there is no statutory protection available, but note that a common-law action for "passing off" of goodwill may apply where someone seeks to benefit from another's good name (*Williamson* v *Meikle* (1909)).

Absolute grounds for refusal

In order to be registered, the trade mark must not fall within the grounds for the refusal of a registration. Thus, by virtue of s 3 of the 1994 Act, the trade mark must have a distinctive character, it must not be descriptive of the underlying goods or services which it represents and it must not represent a customary articulation of the trade. Moreover, it is provided in s 3(2) and (3) of the 1994 Act that a sign must not be registered as a trade mark if it consists exclusively of the shape (or another characteristic) which results from the nature of the goods themselves, the shape (or another characteristic) of goods which is necessary to obtain a technical result, or the shape (or another characteristic) which gives substantial value to the goods.

Registration of a trade mark will be refused if it is contrary to public policy or to accepted principles of morality or it is of such a nature as to deceive the public as to the nature, quality or geographical origin of the goods or service. There are also restrictions in relation to matters that are contrary to general law and then in particular relation to the protection of designations of origin or geographical indications, traditional terms for wine or traditional specialities guaranteed, and plant varieties. Provision is also made for specially protected emblems, and a standalone provision that bad faith applications shall not be registered.

Relative grounds for refusal

In addition to those absolute grounds, s 5 of the 1994 Act also provides for certain relative grounds for the refusal of registration of the trade mark. First, a trade mark must not be registered if it is identical with an earlier trade mark and the goods or services for which the trade mark is applied for are identical with the goods or services for which the earlier trade mark is protected. Second, registration will be refused where the mark is identical with an earlier trade mark and is to be registered for goods or services similar to those for which the earlier trade mark is protected or where the mark is similar to an earlier trade mark and is to be registered for goods or services identical with or similar to those for which the earlier trade mark is protected and, in both circumstances, there exists a likelihood of confusion on the part of the public, which includes the likelihood of association with the earlier trade mark. Third, a trade mark will be refused registration where it is identical with or similar to an earlier trade mark if or to the extent that the earlier trade mark has a reputation in the UK and the use of the later mark without due cause would take unfair advantage of, or be detrimental to, the distinctive character or repute of the earlier trade mark. This ground applies irrespective of whether the goods and services for which the trade mark is to be registered are identical with, similar to or not similar to those for which the earlier trade mark is protected. Next, a trade mark must be refused registration in situations where certain earlier rights are in play. This will be the case if its use in the UK is liable to be prevented by virtue of any rule of law (for example, the law of passing off) which protects an unregistered trade mark or other sign used in the course of trade and the rights to the unregistered trade mark or other sign were acquired prior to the date of application for registration of the trade mark or date of the priority claimed for that application. There is also special provision for protection of designations of origin or geographical indications that can apply where this is relevant, and a catch-all for earlier rights other than those referred to above, in particular by virtue of the law of copyright or industrial property rights.

Registration

In the UK, an application for registration of a trade mark is made with the UKIPO. The UKIPO will examine for earlier UK trade marks or international trade marks protected in the UK which conflict with the application. If such conflicting marks are identified, the applicant and the prior registrants will be notified. The applicant then has the right to choose whether to continue with their application, to alter it or to seek the approval of the prior registrant to the application. Sections 42 and 43 of the Trade Marks Act 1994 stipulate that a registered trade mark receives protection from conflicting registrations and infringement for a period of 10 years, which may be renewed for further periods of 10 years. For example, the first ever trade mark registered in 1876 has been renewed many times and is still on the Register today.

Protection from infringement

Section 10 of the 1994 Act deals with the infringement of registered trade marks. It is stated that a person infringes a registered trade mark if he uses in the course of trade a sign which is identical with the trade mark in relation to goods or services which are identical with those for which it is registered. Section 10(2) of the 1994 Act builds on s 10(1) to the effect that a person infringes a registered trade mark if he uses in the course of trade a sign where, because the sign is identical with the trade mark and is used in relation to goods or services similar to those for which the trade mark is registered or the sign is similar to the trade mark and is used in relation to goods or services identical with or similar to those for which the trade mark is registered, there exists a likelihood of confusion on the part of the public, which includes the likelihood of association with the trade mark. A person also infringes a registered trade mark if he uses a sign in the course of trade which is identical to or similar to the trade mark, where the trade mark has a reputation in the UK and the use of the sign (without due cause) takes unfair advantage of, or is detrimental to, the distinctive character or the repute of the trade mark; this is the case irrespective of whether the goods and services in relation to which the sign is used are identical with, similar to or not similar to those for which the trade mark is registered. A relevant case on this point is *William Grant & Sons Irish Brands Ltd* v *Lidl Stiftung & Co KG* (2021), where a supermarket was found to have breached the trade mark of a gin producer with its discount brand that featured a similar label and bottle to that of the gin producer. Infringement can also take place in relation to packaging, labels, tags, security or authenticity features or devices, or any other means to which a trade mark is affixed for goods or services. There are also provisions about a trade mark holder's entitlements to prevent goods entering the UK without being released for free circulation and to take action against an agent or representative who registers a trade mark in their name without consent. However, in terms of s 11 of the 1994 Act, where an individual uses a registered trade mark in accordance with honest practices in industrial or commercial matters, the trade mark is not infringed where that person uses their own name or address. Similarly, there is no infringement by the use of signs or indications which are not distinctive or which concern the kind, quality, quantity, intended purpose, value, geographical origin, the time of production of goods or of rendering of services, or other characteristics of goods or services, or by use which is for the purpose of identifying or referring to goods or services as those of the proprietor of that trade mark, in particular where that use is necessary to indicate the intended purposes of a product or service, for example as accessories or spare parts. This section entitles a rival trade to engage in comparative advertising, provided that the use complies with the requirements of "honest practices".

Remedies for infringement

Section 14 of the 1994 Act regulates the raising of actions for infringement. If successful, the remedies of damages, interdict, count, reckoning and payment, and all other usual remedies in relation to the infringement of property rights are available to the successful trade mark owner. The court also has the power under s 15 of the 1994 Act to order the erasure, removal or obliteration of the offending sign or the destruction of the infringing goods, articles or material where such erasure, removal or obliteration is not reasonably practicable. Finally, by virtue of the provisions of s 16 of the 1994 Act, a trade mark owner may apply to the court for an order for the delivery to them of any infringing material or articles which a person has in their possession, custody or control in the course of a business.

DESIGN RIGHTS

Design rights may be protected under CDPA or the Registered Designs Act 1949 (the "1949 Act"). In the latter case, the design is registered, whereas in the former it is not. Design rights arise by operation of law without registration under CDPA. Section 213(2) of CDPA directs that "design" means the design of the shape or configuration (whether internal or external) of the whole or part of an article. Thus, there is no requirement to demonstrate that the design is appealing to the eye in any way. Registered designs under the 1949 Act are much stronger than CDPA in the protection that they afford designers. Section 1 of the 1949 Act directs that the extent of the protection of the "design" is wide enough to encompass the appearance of the whole or a part of a product resulting from the features of, in particular, the lines, contours, colours, shape, texture or materials of the product or its ornamentation. Section 1B of the 1949 Act goes on to stipulate that the design must be new (in the sense that no identical design or no design whose features differ only in immaterial details has been made available to the public before the relevant date) and possess individual character (by which is meant that the overall impression it produces on the informed user differs from the overall impression produced on such a user by any design which has been made available to the public before the relevant date, taking into account the degree of freedom of the author in creating the design). This can be understood in terms of a requirement that the design must be appealing to the eye in order to be eligible for registration under the 1949 Act. Thus, in terms of s 1C of the 1949 Act, a design which is solely dictated by the nature of its technical function will not be registrable under the 1949 Act.

Essential Facts

- The main types of intellectual property right which are recognised by the law are copyright, patents, trade marks and designs.
- Copyright may exist in literary, dramatic, musical or artistic works, films, broadcasts, sound recordings and typographical arrangements of published works.
- There is a requirement that the literary, dramatic, musical or artistic work be "original" and "recorded, in writing or otherwise" in terms of ss 1(1)(a) and 3(2) of CDPA.
- The right of copyright consists of two components, namely the economic right and the moral right.
- A patent may be granted only for an invention in respect of which certain conditions are satisfied, namely that the invention is new, involves an inventive step, and is capable of industrial application; and its commercial exploitation must not be contrary to public policy or morality.
- A trade mark is any sign capable of being represented graphically which is capable of distinguishing goods or services of one undertaking from those of other undertakings.
- Design rights may be protected under CDPA or the Registered Designs Act 1949.

Essential Cases

University of London Press Ltd v University Tutorial Press Ltd (1916): held that exam papers would attract copyright protection as "original literary works".

10 DILIGENCE

Where an unsecured creditor provides a service or supplies goods to a debtor and raises an invoice, in an ideal world, the creditor would be ensured that payment is forthcoming without taking any action. In most cases, this is what will happen. But not always. Where a debtor fails to pay, there are different legal options available to an unsecured creditor. One of these is to petition for the sequestration or liquidation of the debtor, that is, to seek to bankrupt the debtor (a process described in Chapter 11). Needless to say, this is fairly extreme. Another option is to do diligence over the assets of the debtor in order to secure payment of the invoice. Diligence is a term used in Scots law to describe a number of methods of enforcing debts in relation to a debtor's assets, and is also used to describe the rights that creditors obtain in those assets arising from such enforcement. There are a number of diligences available to an unsecured creditor and they each involve a judicial process. When completed, diligence ordinarily amounts to a judicial form of security: that is, a right in security in favour of the unsecured creditor over the assets of the debtor under judicial supervision.

Diligence is an area that has been much affected by statute. Relevant legislation includes the Debtors (Scotland) Act 1987 (the "1987 Act"), the Debt Arrangement and Attachment (Scotland) Act 2002 (the "2002 Act") and the Bankruptcy and Diligence etc (Scotland) Act 2007 (the "2007 Act"). The 2007 Act made a number of reforms, some of which are in force but some of which have never been introduced.

THE TYPES OF DILIGENCE AVAILABLE

There are four principal forms of diligence. These four diligences can be best understood by dividing them into two camps: first, according to the type of property over which they are available; and, second, in accordance with the nature of the action taken over the property, that is, whether it entitles the creditor to *freeze* the debtor's use of the property or whether it enables them to *seize* that asset from the debtor. The particular types of diligence are discussed further below.

Contrast with bankruptcy

Diligence can be contrasted with the bankruptcy (sequestration) process. Unlike diligence, bankruptcy is a procedure which seeks to protect all of the debtor's creditors. In the case of bankruptcy, all of the assets of the debtor (subject to limited exceptions) are vested in the trustee and the distribution of funds by the trustee is undertaken on the basis of equality: that is, the *pari passu* principle applies. Another difference is that bankruptcy entails the involvement of a third party in the process, known as a trustee, whereas diligence involves no intermediary. Thus, in contrast with bankruptcy, diligence is a particularly self-interested process which enables one unsecured creditor to secure an advantage over the other unsecured creditors of the debtor and for that reason it is akin to a right in security, albeit under the auspices of judicial supervision.

Attachment

The first diligence to mention is attachment, which is used against corporeal moveable assets. Attachment replaced the diligence known as poinding. Attachment ultimately leads to the sale of the debtor's property. The proceeds of sale are then applied by the creditor towards the repayment of the debts owed by the debtor to the creditor. As will become apparent, certain corporeal moveables are exempted from the diligence of attachment. The relevant legislation governing attachment is contained in Pt 2 of the 2002 Act (as amended by Pt 13 of the 2007 Act).

Arrestment

Arrestment is available over corporeal and incorporeal moveable assets: for example, ships and cargo owned by the debtor; the goods of the debtor held in the hands of a third party; the funds of the debtor held by a bank in a bank account; and the earnings of a debtor held by the debtor's employer.

Inhibition

The third diligence to mention is inhibition. Inhibition is available over the heritable property of a debtor. It is a "freeze" diligence in the sense that it does not result in the transfer of the debtor's property to the creditor. Instead, it disentitles the debtor from dealing with the inhibited asset. An inhibition can only be exercised by a creditor over the heritable assets of a debtor.

Adjudication

Finally, the diligence of adjudication for debt ("adjudication") must be mentioned. It is now an exceptionally rare form of diligence but may still be used by a creditor. Like inhibition, adjudication can also be exercised over the heritable property of the debtor. However, unlike inhibition, it is a "seize" diligence to the effect that it ultimately entitles the creditor to seize the heritable property of the debtor and vests a real right in the heritable property in the creditor. It should also be noted that adjudication is a residual diligence in Scots law and so can be used for property, such as intellectual property and certain digital assets, for which no other type of diligence is available. The Scottish Parliament has legislated to abolish adjudication (s 79 of the 2007 Act) and, by virtue of ss 81 and 129 of the 2007 Act, it would be replaced by diligences to be known as "land attachment" and "residual attachment", but there is no indication of whether and when the relevant provisions might be brought into force.

Other diligences

The diligence of "money attachment" (ss 174–198 of the 2007 Act) allows diligence on coinage and banknotes and banking instruments. Other diligences known to Scots common law, such as real poinding, and sequestration for rent (see s 208 of the 2007 Act), have been abolished and maills and duties would be abolished in terms of s 207 of the 2007 Act if ss 81–128 of the 2007 Act, introducing the diligence of land attachment, come into force. For that reason, those diligences will not be considered further in this book.

ENFORCEMENT OF DILIGENCE

In order to execute diligence, a creditor requires to prove that a debt exists, perhaps most obviously by obtaining a court decree against the debtor. A creditor then appoints a sheriff officer or messenger-at-arms to execute the diligence. The 2007 Act threatened to abolish sheriff officers and messengers-at-arms and replace them with judicial officers in terms of s 57 of the Act but those provisions were not brought into force. Further aspects regarding enforcement are given in relation to particular diligences below.

PRIORITY AND EFFECT OF DILIGENCE

As explained above, diligences executed over the assets of the debtor rank in accordance with the date of execution of diligence in accordance with the *prior tempore potior jure* principle (see Erskine, *Institute*, III, 6, 1). Thus, it is important to stress that the priority of diligences is dictated neither by the date on which the debt owed by the debtor to the creditor was constituted, nor by the date of the court decree. The effect of a creditor executing diligence over an individual asset of the debtor is such that the creditor is given a real right in security over that asset. However, this is subject to one exception, namely inhibition. It should also be stated that in some contexts the priority of diligences against other rights differs from the general position of priority according to date of execution. Diligence that is "effectually executed" before the attachment (crystallisation) of a floating charge ranks ahead of the charge, even if executed after the charge's creation date (see eg Companies Act 1985, s 463(1)(a), Insolvency Act 1986, s 60(1), and *MacMillan v T Leith Developments Ltd* (2017)). In addition, diligence executed within close proximity to sequestration or liquidation will be rendered ineffective. For example, arrestments and attachments executed within 60 days of the commencement of those processes or thereafter are not effectual to create a preference. There are additional rules in this area; however, these particular rules will not be dealt with in further detail here (see Bankruptcy (Scotland) Act 2016, s 24 and Sch 7 para 1).

It is not possible to execute diligence against a debtor where the asset in question is owned by a third party: for example, where a third party's assets are merely possessed by the debtor in the debtor's home. Where a third party enjoys some right in the property of the debtor, the interaction between those third-party rights and the diligence requires to be examined. The nature of the third-party right and the diligence affects the outcome. First, where the asset is co-owned by the debtor and a third party, the diligence is subject to the rights of the co-owner. Second, where a third party is the holder of a subordinate real right (in other words, a real right other than ownership) over the individual asset such as a real right in security, lease or servitude, that real right is unaffected by the diligence provided it was constituted prior to that diligence. Third, with the exception of inhibition, the personal rights of third parties over the assets of the debtor are defeated: for example, where a debtor enters into a contract to sell an asset to a third party and diligence is executed over that asset, the rights of the third party to have that asset conveyed to them are defeated, even in circumstances where the third party has paid the purchase price. Finally, it is not possible for the debtor's personal creditors to execute diligence over assets owned by the debtor which are held in trust for a beneficiary (*Heritable Reversionary Co Ltd v Millar* (1892)).

ATTACHMENT

Introduction

The first diligence to consider is attachment, which replaced the historic diligence of poinding. It is recognised as a form of diligence which is available over corporeal moveable property for recovery of money owed in terms of s 10(1) of the 2002 Act. In order to be effective, attachment must follow an execution of a decree or a document of debt and only upon property owned (whether alone or in common) by the debtor. Attachment is only competent where the debtor has been served with a charge for payment, the period for payment specified in the charge has expired without payment being made, and, where the debtor is an individual, the creditor has, no earlier than 12 weeks before taking any steps to execute the attachment, provided the debtor with a debt advice and information package.

Restricted articles

Section 11 of the 2002 Act stipulates certain articles which cannot be attached (for example, the debtor's tools of trade, books, vehicles reasonably required (where the value does not exceed specified amounts), garden tools, etc), and attachment (under s 12) cannot be conducted on Sundays or public holidays or before 8 am or after 8 pm. If the debtor's assets are contained within their dwellinghouse, Pt 3 of the 2002 Act provides that a creditor must first obtain an exceptional attachment order before attaching non-essential assets, which are corporeal moveable property belonging to the debtor that are kept in a dwellinghouse, but excluding certain items. The excluded items include reasonably required clothing, medical aids, medical equipment, children's toys, articles reasonably required for the care or upbringing of a child, beds, bedding, household linen, chairs, settees, tables and lights reasonably required and other materials itemised in Sch 2 to the 2002 Act. As the name suggests, exceptional attachment will only be available to a creditor in extreme circumstances and where attempts have already been made to recover in other ways.

Procedure

In executing an attachment, a sheriff officer is entitled to presume that the debtor owns any item in the possession of the debtor, under the terms of s 13 of the 2002 Act, although enquiries must be made of any person at the place where the article is situated. Section 13A provides that immediately after executing an attachment, an attachment schedule must be given to the debtor or, if that is not practicable, left at the place where the attachment was executed.

In the event that the assets are located outwith the dwellinghouse of the debtor, or within mobile homes which are not the only or principal residence of the debtor, a special procedure exists in terms of ss 14–19 of the 2002 Act. The procedure enables sheriff officers to open lockfast places. Moreover, in terms of s 19A of the 2002 Act, a procedure exists which entitles sheriff officers to remove certain assets from the debtor's property

without notice for security or if it is necessary to do so to preserve the value
of the asset. An attachment must be reported to the court and the debtor
is entitled to make payment to have the attached articles redeemed. Where
the debtor fails to pay, the creditor has the power to remove the assets and
have them publicly auctioned.

Interim attachment

Section 9A of the 2002 Act enables the court to grant warrant for diligence
by attachment of corporeal moveable property owned (whether alone or in
common) by the debtor on the dependence of an action: that is, where the
creditor raises an action or proceedings against the debtor, it is possible for
the creditor to exercise attachment over an asset or assets of the debtor in
security of the action. If the action fails, the diligence will also be rendered
ineffective. Such attachment is known as interim attachment. Section 9A(2)
of the 2002 Act directs that a warrant for interim attachment is competent
only where an action contains a conclusion for payment of a sum other
than by way of expenses.

Restricted articles

Like attachment, there are various restrictions on the articles which can be
subjected to interim attachment and these are specified in s 9B of the 2002
Act: for example, any article within a dwellinghouse, a mobile home which
is the only or principal residence of a person other than the debtor, any
article of a perishable nature or which is likely to deteriorate substantially
and rapidly in condition or value, and any article acquired by the debtor to
be sold by the debtor or as a material for a process of manufacturing for sale
by the debtor, in the ordinary course of that trade.

ARRESTMENT

The next diligence to consider is arrestment. Arrestment may be in execution or on the dependence of an action. Arrestment is a diligence which is
available over the moveable assets of the debtor, and is ordinarily used for
incorporeal property. The most common assets of the debtor to be arrested
are bank accounts and shares. The creditor is referred to as the "arrester",
the debtor is often known as the "common debtor" and the final party is
the "arrestee" (ie the party who owes obligations to the common debtor,
against whom the common debtor has certain rights and in whose hands
the arrestment is made). Thus, the diligence of arrestment involves three
parties – the creditor/arrester, the common debtor and the arrestee (the

debtor of the common debtor) – and in that sense it is tripartite in nature. The term "common debtor" serves to distinguish the debtor of the enforcing creditor from the third-party arrestee, as it can be seen that both these parties are debtors. In the case of competing arrestments, the *prior tempore potior jure* principle applies.

Procedure

The procedure for initiating the diligence of arrestment is set out in s 73A of the Debtors (Scotland) Act 1987 (the "1987 Act"). It is provided that an arrestment in execution must follow a decree in respect of the debt due to the creditor and a schedule of arrestment must be served upon the debtor. The service of a schedule of arrestment on the debtor serves to attach all of the assets listed on the schedule in favour of the arrester. Section 73E of the 1987 Act provides that the arrestment attaches the lesser of (a) the sum due by the arrestee to the debtor or (b) the sum due by the debtor to the arrester, plus expenses, and interest. Thus, it is not possible for a creditor to arrest more than the principal sum, plus interest and expenses, which it is due from the debtor.

Effect on incorporeal moveables

When the incorporeal moveable assets of the debtor are arrested, they are effectively frozen and the debtor is unable to deal with those assets. If the arrestee also holds corporeal moveables as well as funds, the arrestment will attach the moveables if the funds are insufficient. The incorporeal moveables are frozen in the sense that when a creditor arrests the bank account of the debtor, the debtor is unable to deal with the funds in that account, for example to withdraw those funds. Under section 73F of the 1987 Act, a prescribed minimum balance of an individual's bank account cannot be arrested. Moreover, it should be recalled that the amount arrested cannot exceed the value of the debt due to the creditor/arrester.

Automatic release

Funds arrested are automatically released from the arrestee to the creditor after 14 weeks from the service of the decree upon the debtor or the date of arrestment in terms of s 73J of the 1987 Act. However, there is an exception which applies where an objection is made. In such a case, ss 73L, 73M and 73N of the 1987 Act direct that a court hearing must take place. The debtor will also be entitled to object to the arrestment under s 73Q of the 1987 Act on the basis that it is unduly harsh. A court hearing must then take place in accordance with s 73R of the 1987 Act.

Furthcoming

Before the expiry of the 14-week period, an arrestment may be enforced by an action for furthcoming. Furthcoming serves to convey ownership of the assets arrested from the arrestee to the arrester, ie to seize the arrested assets. Section 95A of the 1987 Act directs that an action for furthcoming must be pursued within a period of 3 years of the date of arrestment.

Other property which can be arrested

Other incorporeal moveable assets of the debtor such as shares and debts/receivables due to the debtor may also be arrested and acquired by furthcoming. A prime example is rent due to a debtor who is a landlord; in such a case, the arrester may arrest in the hands of the tenant. However, it is not possible to arrest money, such as bank notes and coins. Instead, money attachment is available for these purposes.

Arrester's rights

When the arrester arrests the incorporeal moveable assets of the debtor, the arrester can obtain no better rights to the assets than the debtor had and so the arrester takes such assets subject to any encumbrances. Thus, if the debtor has granted a right in security over those assets to a third party, the arrester's rights in the assets arrested are taken subject to the rights of the secured third party. Conversely, the arrestment cannot operate to make the arrester's position worse than if they had not arrested.

Acquirenda

The general rule is that *acquirenda* cannot be arrested, that is, things or rights acquired by the debtor after the time of arrestment (Erskine, *Institute*, III, 6, 18–19). The effect of this rule is that where a bank account with no funds is arrested on 16 February 2022, this is ineffective to arrest funds which are credited to the common debtor's account on 17 February 2022. However, *acquirenda* and future debts should be neither conflated nor confused. It is possible to arrest future debts, that is, debts which presently exist, but which are not due to be paid until some date in the future (*Stair Memorial Encyclopaedia*, vol 8, para 268). The classic example is contractual sums due to be paid under a loan agreement. Moreover, an arrestment catches only the existing asset arrested. For example, if an arrester on day 1 arrests the common debtor's bank account and there is a balance of £1,000, this is arrested. However, if

£50,000 is credited to the common debtor's bank account on day 2, this is not arrested.

Effect of arrestment

There are two competing theories regarding the effect of an arrestment: that is, Scots law is unclear as to which theory applies. The first theory is that an arrestment acts as a signal to the arrestee which prohibits the arrestee from transferring the asset to the debtor: that is, the arrestee is prohibited from enabling the debtor to receive or deal with the asset(s) arrested. Thus, this first theory is known as the "prohibition theory" (see *Lord Advocate* v *Royal Bank of Scotland* (1977) and *Iona Hotels Ltd* v *Craig* (1990)). The second theory is referred to as the "attachment theory". In terms of the attachment theory, an arrestment is something more than a simple instruction to the arrestee prohibiting them from enabling the debtor to deal with the arrested assets. Instead, the effect of an arrestment is to set down a nexus on the subject arrested. In the case of funds arrested, an arrestment is tantamount to a conditional assignation of the funds to the arrester, which condition will be purified when the process of furthcoming or equivalent is effectively completed in the future. On the other hand, an arrestment of goods is treated as if the arrester has been conferred with a real right in security over those arrested goods (see *Lindsay* (1860) and *Inglis* (1898)). In many cases, the difference in analysis between the prohibition and attachment theories will not affect the outcome in practical terms; however, in complex cases, particularly involving the ranking of arrestments, the outcome may diverge depending on which theory is applicable.

Multiplepoinding

Multiplepoinding is an institution separate from arrestment and arises where the holder of a fund of money or property, known as a fund *in medio*, is the subject of a number of competing claims from creditors. The process enables the arrestee (ie the holder of the fund) to place matters in the hands of the court. A pre-condition to doing so is that there have been multiple arrestments of the same funds or property in the hands of the arrestee. The court then deals with the claims and directs how such funds should be applied.

Arrestment of goods

Arrestment of goods can be used in circumstances where the goods of the debtor are held by a third party: for example, in a warehouse or storage facility.

1

58 SCOTTISH COMMERCIAL LAW

INHIBITIONS

Inhibition is a diligence which is available to a creditor over the heritable property of the debtor. When effected, the diligence covers the entirety of the debtor's heritable property. An inhibition is not effective to confer a real right in favour of the creditor. The rights which are given to a creditor are determined by common-law rules and the 2007 Act. The new statutory rules are properly classified as reform to the common law rather than a new statutory code which necessarily excluded the underlying common law (*Playfair Investments Ltd* v *McElvogue* (2013)). In essence, an inhibition is a "freeze" diligence (ie the inhibited property is deemed litigious) but does not transfer title in the heritable property to the creditor or give them a real right in security.

Procedure

Inhibitions can be used to enforce decrees or documents of debt. Where the debtor is an individual an inhibitor is under an obligation to serve a debt advice and information package upon the debtor along with a schedule of inhibition before an inhibition becomes effective. The 2007 Act removed the need for a letter issued under the Signet of the Court of Session, known as letters of inhibition.

Section 149 of the 2007 Act introduced a new version of s 155 of the Titles to Land Consolidation (Scotland) Act 1868 to the effect that an inhibition takes effect from the beginning of the day on which it is registered in the Register of Inhibitions. However, this is subject to an exception which is applicable in circumstances where a notice of inhibition is registered in advance, the schedule of inhibition is served on the debtor after that registration, and the inhibition is registered within 21 days thereof. In these circumstances, the inhibition has effect from the beginning of the day on which the schedule of inhibition is served. In terms of s 148 of the 2007 Act, an inhibition is registered only by registering a schedule of inhibition and the certificate of execution of the inhibition in the Register of Inhibitions under the debtor's name.

Effect of inhibition

In terms of s 160 of the 2007 Act, the debtor is precluded from selling or alienating the heritable property which he owns or granting a deed which affects the property, including granting a security right. This is subject to the exception in s 159 of the 2007 Act that purchasers in good faith who acquire the property for adequate consideration will not be affected by the inhibition. Subject to s 159, the effect of any contravention on the part of the debtor is that the alienation is voidable at the behest of the inhibitor: that is, it is not automatically void from the outset. The inhibitor has the ability to reduce (ie annul) the conveyance only in a limited sense. If a disposition or heritable security is granted by the debtor contrary to the inhibition, this disposition or security is still good against other parties. The reduction will, however, mean that an inhibitor continues to have the ability to obtain an adjudication in relation to such property (see further below).

Ranking of inhibitions

Section 154 of the 2007 Act stipulates that an inhibition no longer confers a preference in any sequestration, insolvency proceedings or other process in which there is ranking. The case of *MacMillan* v *T Leith Developments* (2017), involving an inhibition in competition with an earlier floating charge but which secured post-inhibition sums, provides details of the earlier legal position, as the inhibition was executed prior to the 2007 Act. The inhibition was held to give priority over the floating charge in a receivership for the sums in question; however, this would no longer be the case due to the existence of s 154 of the 2007 Act. Nevertheless, the precise effects of s 154 are not entirely clear, such as in the context of a ranking competition between an inhibition and a later floating charge or standard security. An inhibitor would generally need to obtain an adjudication or other diligence in order to have a priority in a ranking process.

Future voluntary acts

It is important to stress that an inhibition only strikes down the future voluntary acts of the debtor. Where a notice of inhibition is registered in the Register of Inhibitions on the same day that the debtor has concluded missives to sell heritable property, any subsequent transfer of property in implementation of the missives is deemed voluntary and so affected by the inhibition. This is because the effect of s 155 of the Titles to Land Consolidation (Scotland) Act 1868 (as amended) is that an inhibition generally takes effect from the beginning of the day on which it is registered (unless a notice of inhibition has been pre-registered, up to 21 days before the inhibition, in which case the date on which a schedule of inhibition was served on the debtor pursuant to that notice is taken as the date of effect). In the case of a sale of heritage by a heritable creditor, an inhibition does not prevent such a sale. In order to profit from the inhibition, the inhibitor must either (1) have adjudged before the date of sale or (2) have arrested the free proceeds after that date. Inhibitions prescribe in terms of s 44 of the Conveyancing (Scotland) Act 1924 after 5 years and they have no effect on any heritage acquired after the date of their registration in terms of s 157 of the Titles to Land Consolidation (Scotland) Act 1868.

ADJUDICATION AND LAW REFORM

As mentioned above, adjudication is used principally for land but also serves as a residual diligence. Its rarity has also been noted and this is in part due to its archaic aspects and practical issues. The focus here will be on adjudication in relation to land. An action for adjudication may follow an inhibition. It is an action which must be raised in the Court of Session and the court's decree must be registered in the Land Register. Unlike an inhibition, adjudication is a "seize" diligence. The debtor retains ownership of the heritable property but the adjudication confers a judicial right in security in favour of the adjudger. The effect is that the creditor is unable to convey the heritage but has the power to evict the debtor from the property and have it let out to a third party. Where the property has already been let by the debtor to a third party, the adjudger is entitled to the rents on the basis of what is referred to as "maills and duties". In terms of ranking, adjudications generally rank according to the date of their registration.

Acquisition of ownership

Where the debt remains unpaid for a period of 10 years, the adjudger has the power to acquire ownership of the property by obtaining a declarator from the court (known as "declarator of expiry of the legal"). However, in reality, this is unlikely to happen, since the debtor may pay beforehand, the rents obtained may pay off the debt, another heritable creditor may sell the property or the debtor may be sequestrated or liquidated. If an adjudger does acquire ownership, they must account to the debtor for any value of the property in excess of the outstanding debt plus expenses (*Hull* v *Campbell* (2011)).

Law reform

If ss 79–128 of the 2007 Act come into force, they will modify the legal position. Section 79 of the 2007 Act stipulates that the diligence of adjudication will be abolished. If abolished, it will be replaced by two new diligences, namely land attachment and residual attachment. Since these provisions are not in force, they will not be considered here.

DILIGENCE ON THE DEPENDENCE AND INTERIM DILIGENCES

In discussing the diligences so far, it has been assumed that they were being pursued by a creditor in execution – that is to say, that a proven liquid debt is owed by the debtor to the creditor doing diligence in execution, for example where the debt is admitted by the debtor and the creditor has already secured a decree from the court which recognises the existence of that debt. However, it is also possible for a creditor to do diligence on the dependence of an action. In such a case, the creditor pursuing an action does not have a decree from the court. Instead the diligence is sought as part of a pursuer's court action and has effect as soon as the action is initiated. Unless it is recalled, the diligence remains in place throughout the process of the court action. Essentially, the property attached by the diligence on the dependence acts as security for the sums claimed by the pursuer under the principal court action – if the pursuer is successful in their court action, those funds or property attached will then be available to satisfy the claim.

Arrestment and inhibition on the dependence

Section 15D of the 1987 Act stipulates that the diligences of arrestment and inhibition may be sought by a pursuer on the dependence of an action or a petition. However, an arrestment on the dependence is not competent in the case of earnings. If the pursuer is successful in their court action and is awarded a decree from the court, the diligence transforms from a diligence on the dependence into a diligence in execution. But if the action is unsuccessful, the diligence on the dependence is of no effect. While the action is in process, it is not possible for furthcoming to be undertaken in respect of an arrestment on the dependence and there is no automatic release of funds.

Criteria for grant

The court will grant an arrestment or inhibition on the dependence of an action in the event that the criteria specified in s 15E(2) (on the basis of no court hearing, although, if an order is made, a date for a hearing under s 15K must be fixed) or s 15F(3) (on the basis of a court hearing) of the 1987 Act are satisfied. That is to say, diligence on the dependence will be granted by the court if (1) the creditor has a *prima facie* case on the merits of the action, (2) there is a real and substantial risk that enforcement of any decree by the creditor would be defeated or prejudiced by the debtor's insolvency, near insolvency or the debtor removing, disposing of, burdening, concealing or otherwise dealing with their assets, and (3) it is reasonable in all the circumstances, having regard to the effect granting the arrestment or inhibition on the dependence may have on any person having an interest in the assets. The burden of proof falls on the pursuer to satisfy the court that the above criteria have been satisfied. In terms of s 15K of the 1987 Act, a debtor can apply for a recall or restriction of diligence on the dependence, thus preventing the process from adversely affecting an individual unduly before the existence of a liquid debt is proved.

Interim attachment

Section 173 of the 2007 Act (introducing ss 9A–9S into the 2002 Act) provides for a new diligence on the dependence, known as interim attachment (mentioned above). Interim attachment is available in respect of the corporeal moveable assets of the debtor, subject to certain excepted assets which broadly mirror those exempt from the diligence of attachment in execution. The criteria which the court must apply as a means of forming a decision whether to grant a warrant for interim attachment reflect the same criteria which are applicable in the context of an arrestment or inhibition on the dependence of an action (see above).

Essential Facts

- Diligences may be classified into those which enable a creditor to *freeze* the debtor's use of the property or *seize* that property from the debtor.
- For the purposes of the ranking of diligences, the *prior tempore potior jure* principle generally applies.
- The principal diligences known to the law of Scotland are attachment, arrestment, inhibition and adjudication (albeit that adjudication may one day be replaced by land attachment and residual attachment, for which the provisions in the 2007 Act are still not in force).
- Attachment is used to do diligence over the corporeal moveable assets of the debtor.
- Arrestment is available over corporeal and incorporeal moveable assets: for example, ships and cargo owned by the debtor, the goods of the debtor held in the hands of a third party, the funds of the debtor held by a bank in a bank account, and the earnings of a debtor held by the debtor's employer. There are competing views as to whether it is a "freeze" or "seize" diligence.
- Inhibition is available over the heritable property of a debtor. It is a "freeze" diligence.
- An action for adjudication may follow an inhibition.

- Unlike an inhibition, adjudication is a "seize" diligence. It is mainly used for heritable property but is also a residual diligence, available for property that cannot be made subject to other types of diligence. The debtor retains ownership (at least until "expiry of the legal") and the adjudger acquires a judicial right in security.
- The diligences of arrestment and inhibition may be sought by a pursuer on the dependence of an action or a petition and interim attachment may likewise be sought.

Essential Cases

Heritable Reversionary Co Ltd v Millar (1892): it is not possible to execute diligence over assets owned by the debtor which are held in trust for a beneficiary.

Lord Advocate v Royal Bank of Scotland (1977) and **Iona Hotels Ltd v Craig (1990)**: authorities for the "prohibition theory" of arrestment.

Lindsay (1860) and **Inglis (1898)**: an arrestment of goods is treated as if the arrester has been conferred with a real right in security over those arrested goods.

MacMillan v T Leith Developments (2017): provides the meaning of "effectually executed" diligence in relation to the ranking of floating charges in competition with diligences, and discusses the effects of inhibitions and relevant ranking rules.

Hull v Campbell (2011): where an adjudger acquires ownership of property after "expiry of the legal", they must account to the debtor for any value of the property in excess of the outstanding debt plus expenses.

11 PERSONAL INSOLVENCY

The Scots law of personal insolvency regulates the position of individual debtors (and certain other parties) who get into financial difficulties. While the phrase "personal insolvency" is uncertain in its meaning, it is generally taken to refer to the situation where an individual debtor is unable to meet their liabilities to creditors.

APPLICABLE LEGISLATION

The principal legislation which applies to personal insolvency is the Bankruptcy (Scotland) Act 2016 (the "2016 Act"). However, other legislation is also relevant, including the Debt Arrangement and Attachment (Scotland) Act 2002.

Bankruptcy has a bearing on many other areas of private law and commercial law such as property law, the law of diligence, the law of rights in security and trust law. The personal insolvency regime applies to individual living debtors (s 2 of the 2016 Act); however, it is also applicable to deceased debtors, trusts, trading or dissolved partnerships and limited partnerships, bodies corporate (other than companies incorporated under the Companies Acts and limited liability partnerships) and unincorporated bodies such as trade unions and clubs (ss 5 and 6 of the 2016 Act). For other insolvency regimes, although there are many analogies with personal insolvency, reference should be made to specialist texts and applicable legislation (such as the Insolvency Act 1986).

THE DEFINITION OF "INSOLVENCY"

Introduction

In order for an individual to enter into the sequestration process or the law of personal insolvency generally, they must first be "insolvent". There are three types of insolvency.

"Practical insolvency"

The first form of insolvency is practical insolvency. This is generally treated as covering the situation where a debtor is unable to pay their debts as they fall due. Practical insolvency describes the situation where the debtor is experiencing cash flow problems: for example, the debtor has trouble paying their debts when required.

"Absolute insolvency"

For the purposes of the personal insolvency regime, the most relevant concepts are "absolute insolvency" and "apparent insolvency". Section 228(5) of the 2016 Act directs that an individual will be deemed to be "absolutely insolvent" where their total liabilities exceed their total assets. Thus, although an individual is able to pay their debts as they fall due and are experiencing no cash flow difficulties, if they are "balance sheet insolvent", they will be deemed to be absolutely insolvent. The concept of "absolute insolvency" is particularly relevant for the provisions of the 2016 Act and the common law, which confer rights in favour of a trustee in sequestration or the debtor's creditors to challenge certain transactions which the latter entered into prior to the date of their sequestration. These challengeable transactions are referred to as "gratuitous alienations" and will be considered in detail below.

"Apparent insolvency"

The final form of insolvency is "apparent insolvency", which is dealt with by s 16 of the 2016 Act. The concept of "apparent insolvency" is important for the purposes of initiating the process of sequestration. In terms of s 16 of the 2016 Act, apparent insolvency is constituted automatically on the occurrence of the following events:

- where the debtor has been sequestrated or has become bankrupt in any part of the UK;
- where the debtor provides written notice to creditors that they have ceased to pay their debts in the ordinary course of business;
- where the debtor grants a trust deed for the benefit of their creditors;
- where a charge for payment has been served on the debtor and the relevant period for payment stipulated therein has expired without payment by the debtor;
- where a decree of adjudication over any part of the debtor's estate has been granted, either for payment or in security;
- where a debt payment programme under the Debt Arrangement and Attachment (Scotland) Act 2002 has been revoked;
- where a creditor of the debtor owed at least the prescribed amount of £1,500 serves a statutory demand for payment (or demands that the debtor finds security for payment) on the debtor and there is no (1) denial of the debt by the debtor or denial that the sum claimed is immediately payable or (2) payment of the debt (or finding of security for payment) within 3 weeks.

SEQUESTRATION

Introduction

Sequestration describes the process whereby the assets of an insolvent debtor are sold and the proceeds of sale are distributed among their creditors. In terms of the sequestration process, the debtor's estate (subject to certain exceptions) is passed to a duly qualified and authorised third party for realisation and distribution to creditors in accordance with prescribed rules. That third party is referred to as the trustee in sequestration.

Initiation of court-approved sequestration

The process of sequestration is governed by s 2 of the 2016 Act and is commonly initiated by the presentation of a petition to the sheriff court. Section 2(1)(b) of the 2016 Act stipulates that a petition may be presented by (1) a qualified creditor or creditors, if the debtor is apparently insolvent, or (2) a trustee acting under a trust deed (provided certain conditions are met). A qualified creditor is one who, at the date of the presentation of the petition, is a creditor of the debtor in respect of liquid or illiquid debts, whether secured or unsecured, which amount to not less than £5,000. Where the application for sequestration is by a creditor the creditor is obliged to serve the debtor with a debt information and advice package in terms of s 3 of the 2016 Act and s 10(5) of the Debt Arrangement and Attachment (Scotland) Act 2002.

Debtor application procedure

It is possible for a debtor to be sequestrated without the requirement for the presentation of a petition to the court, by way of the debtor application procedure. This enables debtors to apply to the Accountant in Bankruptcy ("AiB") for their own sequestration in terms of s 2(1)(a) of the 2016 Act, as long as conditions in either s 2(2) or s 2(8) are met. Section 2(2) provides the requirements for a minimal asset process (MAP) sequestration, which is for debtors with low income and few assets. Under MAP, the AiB is automatically deemed to be the trustee in sequestration. There are various conditions for a MAP, including (i) the total amount of the debtor's debts is to be not more than £25,000, (ii) the total amount of the debtor's assets must not exceed £2,000, with no single asset exceeding £1,000, (iii) the debtor must have been granted a certificate of sequestration in accordance with s 9, and (iv) in the 5 years prior to the date of application the debtor has not been subject to an award of sequestration nor been subject to an award of sequestration under MAP in the 10 years ending on the day before the day on which the debtor application is made. Section 2(8) applies more generally to debtor applications (ie is used for non-MAP cases) and enables a debtor to make an application to the AiB where (i) the total amount of their debts is not less than £3,000, (ii) an award of sequestration has not been made against them in the period of 5 years ending on the day before the date the debtor application is made, (iii) the debtor has obtained the advice of a money adviser (in accordance with s 4(1)), (iv) the debtor has given a statement of undertakings, and (v) any one of the following three criteria is satisfied:

- the debtor is apparently insolvent;
- the debtor has been granted a certificate for sequestration in accordance with s 9 of the 2016 Act, by a person authorised to grant a certificate; or
- the debtor has granted a trust deed over his estate and the trustee has attempted to make the trust deed protected without success (a trust deed becomes protected under s 163 of the 2016 Act where certain conditions are met, and it thereby becomes generally binding on creditors).

In the remainder of this chapter, consideration of debtor applications will principally be on the procedure arising from s 2(8) cases (ie non-MAP cases), albeit that some of the points made also apply to MAP cases.

Criteria for grant of debtor application procedure

Section 22(1) of the 2016 Act directs that the AiB must award sequestration forthwith if the debtor application is made in accordance with the 2016 Act, the debtor has made the application in compliance with the conditions specified in s 2(8) of the 2016 Act and the debtor has provided a statement of assets and liabilities in accordance with s 8(3)(a). Where the AiB awards sequestration on the making of a debtor application, s 22(7)(a) of the 2016 Act provides that the date of sequestration is the date on which sequestration is awarded.

Criteria for grant of petition for sequestration by the court

Where a petition for sequestration is presented to the sheriff court, the debtor must be given the chance to defend. This is effected by the sheriff granting a warrant to cite the debtor under s 22(3) of the 2016 Act, which calls on the debtor to appear before them to explain why sequestration should not be awarded. Section 23(1) of the 2016 Act directs that the sheriff must refuse to award sequestration if (1) cause is shown why sequestration cannot competently be awarded or (2) the debtor forthwith pays or satisfies, or produces written evidence of the payment or satisfaction of, the debt in respect of which they became apparently insolvent and any other debt due by them to the petitioner and any creditor concurring in the petition. Section 22(5) of the 2016 Act directs the sheriff to make the award of sequestration forthwith if they are satisfied that:

- if the debtor has not appeared, proper citation has been made of the debtor;
- the petition has been presented in accordance with the provisions of the 2016 Act;
- a copy of the petition has been sent to the AiB on the day the petition for sequestration was presented;
- in the case of a petition by a creditor, the requirements of the 2016 Act relating to apparent insolvency have been fulfilled; and
- in the case of a petition by a trustee, the debtor has failed to comply with an obligation or instruction specified in s 2(7)(a) or the petition includes an averment in accordance with s 2(7)(b) of the 2016 Act (ie that it would be in the best interests of the creditors that an award of sequestration be made).

Where the above criteria are fulfilled, the sheriff must award sequestration and the case of *Sales Lease Ltd* v *Minty* (1993) demonstrates that the sheriff has no discretion in the matter. However, in terms of s 23(2) of the 2016 Act, the sheriff has the power to continue the petition for a period of no more than 42 days where the sheriff is satisfied that the debtor will, within 42 days beginning with the day on which the debtor appears before the sheriff, pay or satisfy the debt in respect of which the debtor became apparently insolvent and any other debt due by the debtor to the petitioner and any creditor concurring in the petition.

The date of sequestration

The date of the sheriff's warrant to cite the debtor is critical. It is the "date of sequestration" where sequestration is awarded on the presentation of a petition for sequestration before the sheriff. Section 26 of the 2016 Act stipulates that registration of (1) the court order (in a case where the sheriff has awarded sequestration subsequent to the presentation of a petition) or (2) the AiB's determination of the debtor application awarding sequestration, must be made in the Register of Inhibitions. Moreover, s 26(1) provides that a copy of the court order must be sent to the AiB and any DAS Administrator as defined in the Debt Arrangement Scheme (Scotland)

Regulations 2011 (SSI 2011/141) where the debtor is taking part in a debt payment programme under the Debt Arrangement and Attachment (Scotland) Act 2002.

Sheriff's or AiB's refusal to award sequestration

Where the sheriff decides to refuse the award of sequestration, the petitioner may lodge an appeal against that decision within 14 days in terms of s 27(4) of the 2016 Act. Likewise, where the AiB refuses to award sequestration pursuant to a debtor application, the debtor may apply to the AiB under s 27(5) of the 2016 Act for a review of the refusal. If AiB confirms the refusal, the debtor may within 14 days of the confirmation appeal to the sheriff in accordance with s 27(8) of the 2016 Act.

Recall of award of sequestration

Where the AiB or the sheriff decides to award sequestration, it is not possible to appeal that decision. However, the 2016 Act prescribes a procedure in terms of s 29 which enables the debtor, any creditor, the AiB, the trustee in sequestration or other interested person to present a petition for recall of the sequestration to the sheriff. The sheriff has the power to recall the sequestration in terms of s 30(1) of the 2016 Act if they are satisfied that it is appropriate to do so taking into account all the circumstances of the case, including matters arising after sequestration and certain factors listed in s 30(2) of the 2016 Act.

Effect of appointment of trustee in sequestration

Where the trustee in sequestration is appointed, a decree of appointment is made which has effect in accordance with ss 78 to 88 of the 2016 Act. These are important sections, since they stipulate the assets of the debtor which vest in and can be dealt with by the trustee. Section 78(1) of the 2016 Act directs quite clearly that the effect of the trustee's appointment is to vest the debtor's whole estate in the trustee of sequestration as at the date of sequestration for the benefit of the debtor's creditors. Thus, s 78(1) of the 2016 Act essentially provides for the statutory conveyance of the entirety of the debtor's assets to the trustee. However, this statutory transfer in title is subject to the *tantum et tale* rule which means that defects or limitations in the title of the debtor pass on to the trustee and the trustee can inherit no better title to the debtor's assets than the debtor had himself (*Heritable Reversionary Co Ltd* v *Millar* (1892)). Thus, if the debtor's property was subject to some encumbrance (for example, a lease), the trustee takes title to the asset subject to that encumbrance.

Particular rules for the transfer of debtor's assets

Heritable property

The 2016 Act provides for various exceptions to the general rule that the trustee takes the entire estate of the debtor on the appointment of the trustee in sequestration. While a trustee in sequestration may complete title to the debtor's heritable property following vesting, s 78(3) and (4) of the 2016 Act narrate that the trustee in sequestration is subject to a handicap in perfecting title to the heritable property. It is provided that the trustee will not be able to register title to the debtor's heritage for a period of 28 days beginning with the date of registration of the notice registered in the Register of Inhibitions in accordance with s 26 of the 2016 Act. The 28-day handicap rule helps to offset the effects of *Burnett's Trustee* v *Grainger* (2004). In *Burnett's Trustee*, a trustee in sequestration registered a notice of title to the debtor's heritable property after his appointment. The date of registration of that notice of title preceded the date on which a third-party purchaser from the debtor had registered a disposition of property belonging to the debtor. The prior registration of that notice of title was sufficient to defeat the rights of the third-party purchaser (even though the latter had paid the purchase price to the debtor prior to the date of sequestration and had received the disposition), since the trustee had won the "race to the register". The 28-day rule seeks to ensure that a purchaser of heritable property from the debtor prior to the date of sequestration has a reasonable period of time in which to register the disposition relating to that property.

Moveable property

Section 78(8) of the 2016 Act directs that where delivery, possession or intimation would normally be required to complete the trustee's title to moveables, such delivery, possession or intimation will be deemed to have occurred by operation of law. However, in the case of incorporeal moveables, where some further step is necessary to perfect title (for example, registration in the register of members of a company or the UK Intellectual Property Office in the case of shares or patents respectively), completion of the trustee's title to those assets does not take place until the occurrence of that step (*Cumming's Trustee* v *Glenrinnes Farms Ltd* (1993)). The consequence of this rule is that the trustee's rights may be defeated where a third party registers title to the property before the trustee (*Morrison* v *Harrison* (1876)). Moreover, on the vesting of the debtor's corporeal moveable assets in the trustee in sequestration, any rights to payment relating to such corporeal moveable assets are also acquired by the trustee (for example, a right to hire payments). By contrast, obligations are not transferred to the trustee.

The general rule is that the trustee in sequestration has the option whether to choose to assume obligations by adopting a relevant contract or not (see s 110(1)) of the 2016 Act and *MacDonald's Trustees* v *Cunningham* (1997), which relates to heritable property).

Acquirenda

Assets or rights acquired by the debtor from the date of sequestration until 4 years later automatically vest in the trustee in sequestration under ss 79(5) and 86(4)–(5) of the 2016 Act. This property is often referred to as "*acquirenda*". Section 86(6) of the 2016 Act specifically provides that any person who holds estate vesting in the trustee must convey or deliver it to the trustee. A common example is where a debtor inherits assets or money from a third party. Likewise, free shares issued by a company to a debtor are deemed to be *acquirenda* in terms of the case of *Accountant in Bankruptcy* v *Halifax plc* (1999) and so vest in the trustee. However, s 86(7) of the Act provides that where a person has in good faith and without knowledge of the sequestration conveyed the estate to the debtor or to a third party on the instructions of the debtor, that person incurs no liability to the trustee except to account for any proceeds of the conveyance which are in their hands. Where a third party conveys property or assets to the debtor in circumstances where they are aware of the debtor's sequestration, the case of *Rankin's Trustees* v *H C Somerville & Russell* (1999) is to the effect that the trustee has the right to seek a remedy against that third party, and if the property paid by the third party to the debtor is cash, the trustee's remedy will be to raise a money claim.

Income

The treatment of the debtor's income is governed by s 85 of the 2016 Act, which stipulates that any income which is received by the debtor after the date of sequestration vests in the debtor and does not pass to the trustee. However, there is an exception. Where income generated is derived from estate vested in the trustee, that income transfers to the trustee: for example, rents or equivalent payments which are derived from moveable or heritable property which has vested in the trustee. The case of *Accountant in Bankruptcy* v *Halifax plc* (1999) decided that free shares issued to the debtor are *acquirenda* and not income and so vest in the trustee. Despite the general position on income, it should be noted that where the debtor's income is at a certain level, they will be required to make a contribution to their creditors under ss 89 and 90 of the 2016 Act. When making a debtor contribution order, the AiB must assess the debtor's contribution using the so-called common financial tool but the amount may be set at zero if the debtor's income is insufficient.

Trust assets and other assets

Property which is held in trust by the debtor does not vest in the trustee as a result of s 88(1)(c) of the 2016 Act. Implicit within this rule is the recognition that the debtor's estate may be divided into their personal patrimony and trust patrimony. Section 187 of the Social Security Administration Act 1992 (read with s 122 of the Social Security Contributions and Benefits Act 1992) excludes social security payments from vesting in the trustee. Such payments are treated as if they are inalienable and the rights to such payments remain with the debtor. Meanwhile, certain property is exempt from vesting in terms of s 88(1)(a)–(b) of the 2016 Act. This refers to items which are excluded from the diligence of attachment in s 11 of, and Sch 2 to, the Debt Arrangement and Attachment (Scotland) Act 2002. Such items include the debtor's books, implements, tools of trade or other equipment required for the exercise of their practice or profession, subject to an aggregate maximum of £1,000.

Duties and functions of trustee in sequestration

The key duties and functions of the trustee in sequestration are set out in ss 50, 109, and 126 of the 2016 Act (with an important restriction in relation to the debtor's family home in s 113). The trustee's duties can be divided into two categories. First, the trustee is under an obligation to recover, manage and realise the estate of the debtor. Second, once the trustee has realised a pot of money, the trustee must then distribute those funds among the debtor's creditors according to a statutorily prescribed order. In distributing such funds, s 129(9) of the 2016 Act states that secured creditors will be the first persons to be paid by the trustee to the extent that they are entitled to receive the value of their security before the estate is distributed in accordance with the order in s 129(1) of the 2016 Act. Thereafter, the trustee must apply the proceeds of the debtor's estate towards payment of their outlays and remuneration. In the case of deceased debtors, the funeral expenses are paid out next. Thereafter, the expenses of the creditor who petitioned for sequestration must be paid, followed by sums owed to the preferred creditors (including for ordinary preferred debts and secondary preferred debts). Ordinary preferred debts include the accrued holiday pay of employees of the debtor up to the date of sequestration (for example, where the debtor is a sole trader) and arrears of wages of the debtor's employees up to 4 months before the sequestration date subject to a ceiling of £800 per employee (Bankruptcy (Scotland) Regulations 2014 (SSI 2014/225)). Secondary preferred debts include sums owed by a debtor to HM Revenue and Customs in respect of VAT, PAYE income tax contributions deducted from employee wages and employee National Insurance contributions. Given the nature of these debts, their relevance is likely to be limited to business debtors. Once such preferred creditors have been paid, ordinary (non-preferential) unsecured creditors are paid (followed by any of the secondary and tertiary non-preferential debts specified in s 129A of the 2016 Act). After this, interest on debts between the date of sequestration and date of payment is paid. Finally, postponed creditors are paid.

It is unusual for all ordinary unsecured creditors to be paid in full. It is common for such ordinary unsecured creditors to be paid a percentage of their claim. In such circumstances, each of the ordinary unsecured creditors ranks *pari passu*, that is, they rank equally where there are insufficient funds to pay each of them in full.

Discharge of debtor

Once the debtor's estate has been applied to pay off the creditors, the debtor is discharged and is relieved from any continuing liability to their creditors. This rule holds good even in those circumstances where creditors have not received the full extent of the sums which they were due to be paid or where the sequestration continues and the trustee remains in office. Where the AiB is not the trustee, they may discharge the debtor under s 137 of the 2016 Act provided that at least 12 months have passed since the sequestration was awarded, and they must have received and considered a report from the trustee and any representations from the debtor or creditors. If the AiB is the trustee, the debtor can be discharged under s 138 of the 2016 Act on the AiB's own initiative at any time after the 12-month period has expired. In order to be discharged, it is important that the debtor has co-operated with the trustee. It should also be noted, however, that under a MAP sequestration, s 140 of the 2016 Act provides that a debtor will be automatically discharged after 6 months. A key effect of a discharge of a debtor is that they are discharged of debts due at the date of sequestration, with some exceptions, meaning that they are no longer personally liable for those debts. This is intended to help a bankrupt person make a fresh start. Yet the discharge of the debtor does not automatically reinvest them in their property and the debtor's right to acquire assets subsequent to their discharge is subject to the *acquirenda* rules noted above.

CHALLENGES TO PRIOR TRANSACTIONS

Where the debtor enters into a transaction with a third party prior to their insolvency, the trustee in sequestration may challenge that transaction by recovering any assets transferred to third parties and/or strike down any rights in security granted in favour of third parties. Such prior transactions are known as "challengeable transactions" and may be pursued in terms of the common law or the provisions of the 2016 Act. However, consideration of the law of challengeable transactions will be restricted here to the provisions contained in the legislation. Two types of challengeable transaction under the 2016 Act will be focused on here. As shall be seen, absolute insolvency, that is, where the debtor's total liabilities exceed their total assets (s 228(5) of the 2016 Act) (so that the debtor is "balance sheet insolvent"), is important in determining whether certain transactions are challengeable.

Gratuitous alienations

The first challengeable transaction is known as a "gratuitous alienation" and is governed by s 98 of the 2016 Act. It is a gift or part gift of property or money by the debtor to a third party. A trustee in sequestration, a judicial factor, a creditor of the debtor, or a trustee under a protected trust deed all have the power to challenge a gratuitous alienation. The case of *Accountant in Bankruptcy* v *Brown* (2009) directs that a creditor's right to challenge is an independent right and they may pursue a third party in accordance with the provisions on gratuitous alienations irrespective of decisions taken by the trustee. There is no requirement for the trustee or creditors to demonstrate that the debtor sought to defraud their creditors or that the alienation was entered into with a view to avoiding the effects of bankruptcy.

Criteria for establishment of gratuitous alienation

Section 98 of the 2016 Act directs that there must be an alienation by the debtor. Second, the alienation must involve the transfer of the property or funds of the debtor or the renunciation or discharge of a debtor's claim or right against a third party. Third, (a) the debtor must have been sequestrated, (b) the debtor must have granted a protected trust deed for the benefit of their creditors, or (c) the debtor must have died and within 12 months their estate was sequestrated or their estate was absolutely insolvent at the time of death and a judicial factor was appointed over the estate within 12 months. Fourth, the alienation must have occurred within the periods stipulated in the 2016 Act. The relevant period is 5 years before the date of sequestration, the grant of the trust deed or the date of the death, where the debtor transfers their property to a third party who is an associate of the debtor. An associate is defined by s 229 of the 2016 Act and extends to various parties, including the husband, wife, civil partner, partner (in the sense of a business partnership), employee, employer, brother, sister, uncle, aunt, nephew, niece, lineal ancestor or lineal descendant of the debtor. However, in all other cases where property is transferred, the appropriate period is 2 years before the relevant date of sequestration, the grant of the trust deed or the date of death of the debtor.

The relevant date of alienation

The relevant date for the purposes of determining when the alienation took place is governed by s 98(3) of the 2016 Act. The relevant date is when the alienation becomes completely effectual. The date of alienation in the case of the transfer of moveables is the date of their delivery, and in *Craiglaw Developments Ltd* v *Wilson* (1997) it was held that the relevant date when funds are consigned in court is the date when such consignation takes place. In the context of the conveyance of heritable property, *Accountant in Bankruptcy* v *Orr* (2005) demonstrates that the relevant date is the registration of the transferee's disposition in the Land Register.

Third-party defences

Where the trustee in sequestration or creditor challenges the alienation to the third party, the third party who is seeking to uphold the validity of the alienation has certain defences under s 98(6) of the 2016 Act. The first defence is to the effect that the debtor's liabilities did not exceed their assets: that is, the debtor was not absolutely insolvent, either immediately, or any other time, after the alienation. The second defence permits the third party to uphold the alienation where they can demonstrate that it was for adequate consideration. The final defence open to the third party is that the alienation was a permitted gift. Section 98(6)(c) of the 2016 Act specifies that a birthday gift, Christmas gift, other conventional gift or a charitable gift (not to an associate) are covered, provided that it was reasonable for the debtor to make those gifts having regard to all the circumstances.

"Adequate consideration"

In practice, it is the second defence which features most heavily in the reported cases: that the alienation was given for adequate consideration. This begs the question as to what constitutes "adequate consideration". In the case of *MacFadyen's Trustee* v *MacFadyen* (1994), a mother had purchased a property for her son and she met the running costs of the property. The title to the property was transferred subsequently by the son to the mother for no consideration. When the son became bankrupt, the mother and son sought to uphold the alienation on the basis that the purchase price which she had paid and her contribution to the running costs amounted to adequate consideration. The court disagreed and ruled that the word "consideration" meant something which was given or surrendered in return for something else and had to be something of material or patrimonial value which could be vindicated in a legal process at the time when it was given. On that basis, it was held that the purchase price and the running costs predated the alienation and so could not amount to adequate consideration. A similar case is *Cay's Trustees* v *Cay* (1998) which held that a husband's obligation to aliment his wife could not represent adequate consideration. More recently, the UK Supreme Court considered the meaning of adequate consideration in *MacDonald* v *Carnbroe Estates Ltd* (2020). The case involved corporate insolvency, rather than personal insolvency; however, the statutory provisions on gratuitous alienations are substantially the same. A company encountered serious financial difficulties and sold heritable property for £550,000 in a quick off-market sale, which was significantly below the open market valuation. The court adopted an objective approach to adequate consideration and considered that there was no commercial justification for the sale to take place for such a discounted amount. Consequently, the adequate consideration defence was unsuccessful.

Remedies

Where an action challenging a gratuitous alienation is successful, various remedies are available. Section 98(5) of the 2016 Act stipulates that the court must grant a decree of reduction, a decree restoring the property alienated to the debtor's estate or a decree in respect of such "other redress as may be appropriate". But where a third party has acquired the property in good faith and for value from the transferee, s 98(7) of the 2016 Act states that such person will not be prejudiced. On the face of it, it is unclear what is meant by such "other redress as may be appropriate" in s 98(5)(b) of the 2016 Act. In *MacDonald* v *Carnbroe Estates Ltd* (2020) the UK Supreme Court confirmed that a court does not have a general discretion as to remedies and that the primary remedy is annulling a transaction by reduction or restoration of the property. However, the UKSC, contrary to earlier case law, also held that where a transferee has paid some consideration (but not adequate consideration), a court in some circumstances can take account of the consideration paid in devising an appropriate remedy (eg by requiring the return of that consideration when the transferred property is restored to the debtor's estate).

Unfair preferences

The other transaction which may be challenged by a trustee in sequestration, a judicial factor, a creditor of the debtor or a trustee under a protected trust deed is referred to as an "unfair preference" and is governed by s 99 of the 2016 Act. Section 99 prohibits a debtor from preferring one creditor to the prejudice of the other creditors since it represents a violation of the debtor's duty to treat creditors equally and fairly. Like the law of gratuitous alienations, unfair preferences can be challenged on the basis of the common law or statutory provisions. Section 99 of the 2016 Act directs that a preference which is created in favour of a creditor within 6 months prior to the date of sequestration of the debtor or the date when the debtor grants a trust deed for the benefit of creditors, that has become a protected trust deed, or the date of the debtor's death can be struck down by the court. Preferences include the situation where a debtor pays one creditor before other creditors, grants a security for pre-existing debt in favour of a particular creditor (but not the other creditors), provides assistance to a particular creditor (but not the other creditors) in executing diligence over the debtor's assets or where the debtor enters into a sham sale of moveable property while retaining possession. For obvious reasons, the first example given is the most common in practice, for instance where a debtor arranges to pay a particular favourite creditor even though the date of that creditor's invoice or fee post-dates the invoices or fees of other creditors. Like gratuitous alienations, s 99(4) of the 2016 Act is to the effect that a preference will be deemed to have been created on the date it became completely effectual.

Excluded transactions

Certain transactions may not be challenged by the trustee, creditor or judicial factor. First, where the debtor enters into a transaction in the ordinary course of trade or business and the creditor is not influenced by any belief that the debtor might be insolvent (see s 99(2)(a) and *Nordic Travel Ltd* v *Scotprint Ltd* (1980)). Second, any transaction involving the payment of a debt in cash (including banknotes, bankers' drafts, cheques, coins and bills) where there is no collusion between the debtor and the creditor (for example, where the creditor is aware of the debtor's precarious financial position and arranges payment in order to defeat the interests of the other creditors of the debtor). Finally, any transaction which represents *nova debita* is excluded: that is, where the debtor and creditor are bound by reciprocal obligations.

Remedies

The remedies available to the successful trustee, creditor or judicial factor are reduction, restoration and such other redress as may be appropriate.

FUTURE REGULATION OF PERSONAL INSOLVENCY

Personal insolvency is an area of law that has been the subject of a significant amount of legislative intervention in recent decades. Even in the last couple of years, there have been a number of amendments to the law. For example, certain changes introduced in response to the COVID-19 pandemic have been made permanent and the debt threshold for a creditor to be able to successfully petition for the sequestration of a debtor has been increased. Yet further reform of the law is also anticipated in the coming years. While we cannot be certain as to what the future changes will be, various aspects of statutory debt solutions are currently being reviewed by the Scottish Government.

Essential Facts

- There are three types of insolvency, namely practical insolvency, absolute insolvency and apparent insolvency.
- Sequestration describes the process whereby the assets of an insolvent debtor are sold and the proceeds of sale are distributed among their creditors.
- The trustee in sequestration administers a debtor's estate on sequestration of that debtor.
- The process of sequestration may be initiated by a creditor or other qualified parties presenting a petition to the sheriff court or by debtor application procedure.
- The effect of the trustee in sequestration's appointment is to vest the debtor's whole estate in the trustee as at the date of sequestration for the benefit of the debtor's creditors.
- Certain assets of the debtor are excluded from vesting in terms of the 2016 Act.
- A trustee in sequestration or creditor may challenge certain transactions entered into by the debtor prior to sequestration on the basis that they constitute a gratuitous alienation or an unfair preference.

Essential Cases

Sales Lease Ltd v Minty (1993): where the criteria now found in s 22(5) of the 2016 Act are satisfied, the sheriff must grant an award of sequestration and has no discretion in the matter.

Heritable Reversionary Co Ltd v Millar (1892): on the statutory conveyance of title to the debtor's estate to the trustee (pursuant to s 78 of the 2016 Act), any defects in the title of the debtor pass on to the trustee and the trustee can inherit no better title to the debtor's assets than the debtor had himself.

Burnett's Tr v Grainger (2004): a trustee in sequestration can obtain title to the debtor's heritable property, and win the "race to the register", by registering a notice of title before a third-party purchaser registers their disposition from the debtor, but there has since been legislative intervention to delay the trustee's ability to complete title (see s 78(3)–(4) of the 2016 Act).

Cumming's Tr v Glenrinnes Farms Ltd (1993) and **Morrison v Harrison (1876)**: in the case of incorporeal moveable assets such as shares and patents which require some other step such as registration to perfect title, the trustee's rights may be defeated where a third party registers title to the property before the trustee.

Accountant in Bankruptcy v Halifax plc (1999): bonus shares issued by a company are deemed to be *acquirenda* and not income of the debtor, so they vest in the trustee.

Rankin's Trs v H C Somerville & Russell (1999): where a third party conveys property or assets to the debtor in circumstances where he is aware of the debtor's sequestration, the trustee has a right of recourse against that third party.

Accountant in Bankruptcy v Brown (2009): a creditor's right to challenge a gratuitous alienation is an independent right and where the trustee in sequestration decides not to challenge a gratuitous alienation, a creditor may nevertheless pursue a third party.

Accountant in Bankruptcy v Orr (2005): the date of alienation for the purposes of s 98(3) of the 2016 Act in the case of the transfer of heritable property is the date of registration of the purchaser's disposition in the Land Register.

MacFadyen's Tr v MacFadyen (1994): "consideration" in relation to gratuitous alienations (see now s 98(6)(b) of the 2016 Act) means something which was given or surrendered in return for something else and must be something of material or patrimonial value which could be vindicated in a legal process at the time when it was given.

MacDonald v Carnbroe Estates Ltd (2020): an objective approach to whether consideration is adequate is taken and, although the primary remedy for a gratuitous alienation is annulling a transaction by reduction or restoration of the property, where a transferee has paid some consideration (but not adequate consideration), in certain circumstances a court may take account of the consideration paid in devising an appropriate remedy.

12 COMMERCIAL DISPUTE RESOLUTION

In previous chapters, the various rights and obligations which are enjoyed and owed by parties in commercial and consumer transactions have been charted. Where disputes arise between seller and purchaser, insured and insurer, owner and hirer, etc, about those rights and obligations, litigation in court is available as a means of resolving that dispute. However, it is not the only avenue which is available. The parties may opt to resolve their disputes through a process other than litigation in the courts. It is the purpose of this chapter to provide an exposition of the various dispute resolution mechanisms which are available.

SUMMARY OF PRINCIPAL FORMS OF DISPUTE RESOLUTION PROCESS

The most obvious option for a person seeking to enforce a legal right is to take legal action in the courts, that is, to litigate. The courts are the principal avenue provided by the legal system as a means of enabling a party to vindicate their legal rights. An alternative is for a party to seek to enforce their legal rights through arbitration. Unlike litigation, arbitration is not conducted in a public forum and so for that reason possesses many attractions. However, arbitration is similar to litigation in the sense that the parties may lead evidence and call witnesses before a third party known as the arbitrator (the historic Scots term for that third party being an "arbiter"). Moreover, in the cases of litigation and arbitration, a decision which is legally binding is handed down by a third party (ie the judge in the case of litigation and the arbitrator in the case of arbitration).

Other forms of dispute resolution procedure involve the parties in dispute receiving a legally binding decision, with that legally binding effect stemming from contractual agreement. The most important in the context of commercial law are neutral expert/neutral evaluation and mediation/conciliation. In the case of a neutral expert procedure, the parties submit their dispute to a nominated expert for resolution. The parties commonly opt into this procedure in terms of a contractual provision and it is particularly common for them to do so in circumstances where property such as land, buildings, shares or intellectual property rights require to be valued and there is a dispute between the parties as to the correct figure. Where an expert is appointed, the expert applies their expertise, skill and experience to fix the valuation. Meanwhile, mediation/conciliation is an altogether different dispute resolution process and entails the mediator/conciliator operating in a role as facilitator, concentrating on bringing the parties in dispute towards consensus and resolution. The mediator/conciliator may take an active role in highlighting the strengths and weaknesses in each party's case or may adopt a less intrusive role. Much depends on the context of the dispute and the nature of the training undertaken by the mediator/conciliator. Another sector-specific dispute resolution process is adjudication (not to be confused with the diligence of the same name), under the Housing Grants, Construction and Regeneration Act 1996, which allows for a quick result in construction disputes. This chapter examines litigation and arbitration only.

LITIGATION

Introduction and disadvantages

Litigation is conducted in the courts of law which are constituted by the legal system. Some of the characteristics of litigation operate as disadvantages in the commercial arena. First, the fact that litigation is conducted in the public arena is a particular drawback since commercial organisations will usually be keen to avoid information which is detrimental to their reputation becoming publicly available. It may be damaging to commercial interests for that information to be made public. Second, litigation is usually costly. Third, litigation generally takes a long time to be completed and, during that period, the commercial relationship between the parties may be irretrievably damaged to the point where they are no longer in a position to continue trading with each other. Sometimes this will not be a concern but it will be particularly disadvantageous where there are few alternative traders in the market. Another difficulty with litigation is that, once it has been completed, it will resolve the legal issue which has resulted in the dispute, but it will do nothing to resolve all other commercial issues which may exist between the parties.

Remedies

Before a party engages in litigation, he must be absolutely clear as to the remedy which he is seeking. The remedies available through the courts are count, reckoning and payment (ie a decree ordering someone to pay a debt), damages (ie a decree ordering someone to pay compensation in respect of a person's loss), declarator (a decree which declares a particular state of affairs to exist), specific implement (a decree compelling someone to do something), interdict (a decree compelling someone not to do something) and reduction (a decree denuding a deed or other legal document of legal effect). Moreover, only a court has the power to grant a party diligence on the dependence of an action, inhibition and reduction. Litigation is an option that is always available to the parties in order to enforce their rights. However, this can be contrasted with arbitration, which is only an option where the parties have contracted into arbitration in terms of a contractual agreement.

The courts and procedures

In Scotland, commercial disputes may be litigated in the sheriff court or the Court of Session.

Sheriff court

Litigation may be pursued in the sheriff court pursuant to ordinary cause or summary cause procedures. Ordinary actions involve the service of an initial writ on the defender in terms of r 3.1 of the Act of Sederunt (Sheriff Court Ordinary Cause Rules) 1993 (SI 1993/1956) ("Ordinary Cause Rules") whereby the defender has 21 days to respond. If the defender fails to provide such a response, the pursuer will be entitled to a decree in absence in terms of r 7 of the Ordinary Cause Rules. Another form of procedure is the simple procedure. Simple procedure was introduced by the Courts Reform (Scotland) Act 2014. A pursuer may raise a civil action pursuant to the simple procedure in terms of the Act of Sederunt (Simple Procedure) 2016 (SSI 2016/200) where the claim is for an amount of no more than £5,000. The simple procedure is designed with party litigants (ie those without legal representation) in mind. However, it is not wholly unusual for pursuers to be represented by qualified legal practitioners. As a result, the sheriff commonly takes a more active role in simple procedure hearings.

Court of Session

Where a case is factually or legally complex, it is not uncommon for the pursuer to initiate a claim in the Court of Session. Section 39 of the Courts Reform (Scotland) Act 2014 provides that the sheriff court has exclusive competence (also known as privative jurisdiction) where the value of the claim is £100,000 or less. Cases above that value may be brought before the Court of Session. The procedures for initiating action in the Court of Session are governed by the Court of Session Rules set out in the Act of Sederunt (Rules of the Court of Session) 1994 (SI 1994/1443). The Court of Session action is raised by the pursuer preparing a document called a summons in the prescribed form. The summons is then signeted if the requisite fee is paid and it meets the requirements of form. Once the summons is signeted, it will be served on the defender. After a period of 21 days, the summons may be lodged with the court for calling and the defender has a short period of 3 days to notify the court that they intend to defend the action by appearing to contest it. The defender has 7 days from the date the summons is called to submit written defences to the court. The defences are then served upon the pursuer and the pursuer has a period of 14 days from the date when the defences were lodged to lodge the open record. The open record is then adjusted by the pursuer and the defender over a period of 8 weeks. After the period of 8 weeks, the record is closed and the pursuer then has a further period of 4 weeks to lodge the closed record. The closed record is the document which draws the summons and the defences together in one document and thus sets out the pleadings of both of the parties to the dispute. The court will fix a proof (a process whereby witnesses and evidence are led), fix a proof before answer (a process whereby witnesses and evidence are led and the case involves a point of law) or schedule a debate on a point of law (which is based on the pleadings in the closed record and in the absence of witnesses and evidence).

Where the subject of the dispute is a matter of commercial law, a spe-cialised commercial action may be raised in the Court of Session. Rule 47.1.2 of the Court of Session Rules directs that a commercial action is an action arising out of, or concerned with, any transaction or dispute of a commercial or business nature. The action does not require to be based on a contract and may include a dispute about leases, construction matters, contracts of sale, insurance, hire-purchase contracts, financial services and other listed matters. The onus falls on the pursuer to seek to have their action dealt with under the commercial action procedure and they may do so by labelling the action as a commercial action in the summons. In a commercial action, the judge plays a very pro-active role in managing the case and is entitled to make a variety of orders. Moreover, the judge is carefully appointed and will commonly have experience in commercial law matters. For that reason, the commercial action procedure is particularly attractive to commercial organisations which are in dispute.

ARBITRATION

Introduction

Although it has a long history, the law of arbitration in Scotland has recently been overhauled by the Arbitration (Scotland) Act 2010 (the "2010 Act"). This replaced the common law and related statutes with a clear code for arbitrating in Scotland. Prior to the 2010 Act's enactment, commercial arbitrations under the UNCITRAL (United Nations Commission on International Trade Law) Model Law (the "Model Law") were provided for by the Law Reform (Miscellaneous Provisions) (Scotland) Act 1990, but this has now been repealed. Parties can still adopt the Model Law as the basis for an arbitration in preference to certain parts of the 2010 Act scheme, but there are mandatory Scottish Arbitration Rules in Sch 1 to the 2010 Act which will continue to operate. This chapter considers the 2010 Act without further reference to the Model Law.

Advantages of arbitration

One of the main benefits of arbitration is that a party has the capacity to appoint as an arbitrator a person who is an expert in the field of the particular commercial dispute. Another key benefit is confidentiality. Administration may also be cheaper than litigation, but that must be considered in light of any venue's or arbitrator's costs that must be met. The procedure is generally more flexible than court procedure and the resolution of the dispute may be brought to a swifter conclusion. In addition, it may be more straightforward to enforce an arbitral award in a foreign jurisdiction than a court decree from a Scottish court.

Reference of matters to arbitration

The parties may refer disputes between themselves to arbitration in terms of a contract. The agreement may be contained in the original contract between the parties or in terms of an arbitration agreement once a dispute arises between them. In terms of s 5 of the 2010 Act, an arbitration agreement is severable from any contract it is contained in and thus can survive any challenge to the wider document. An arbitration seated in Scotland is governed by the Scottish Arbitration Rules contained in Sch 1 to the 2010 Act, subject to any permissible amendments to those rules. Section 8 stipulates which of those rules are mandatory and cannot be modified or disapplied. Rules relating to the jurisdiction of the tribunal are largely mandatory, and thus it is not possible to invoke the jurisdiction of the court in the face of a valid arbitration agreement. This reflects the historical position, whereby if the parties agreed to resolve their dispute by arbitration, the courts would enforce that agreement (*Sanderson v Armour & Co* (1922)). If one of the parties subsequently attempts to litigate the dispute in the courts, the courts will refuse to hear the matter and will refer it to arbitration. Other rules on less fundamental matters, such as expenses and the number of arbitrators, are default rules and can be modified by agreement.

Conduct of proceedings

The nature of the proceedings and their conduct will be governed by the Scottish Arbitration Rules as competently amended.

Involvement of the Court of Session

When an arbitrator resolves a dispute, the common law provided that this was determinative of the fact and law of the dispute in question. Section 3(1) of the Administration of Justice (Scotland) Act 1972 provided an ability for the parties to state a case for the opinion of the Court of Session in respect of any question of law arising from the dispute. This statute has been replaced by r 69 (which is a default rule), allowing a perceived legal error to be challenged at the Court of Session. That challenge is governed by the mandatory r 70. It is also possible to refer a question of law to the Court of Session under r 41.

The award

Once the arbitrator has considered the dispute, he will produce an arbitral award. Part 6 of the Scottish Arbitration Rules sets out the tribunal's powers, which can involve ordering the payment of a sum of money (including damages) or ordering a party to do or refrain from doing something. Awards can only be challenged in accordance with Pt 8, which details grounds such as serious irregularity and (as noted above) legal error. For an example of such a challenge (which in the event was unsuccessful), see *Arbitration Appeal No 4 of 2019* (2020).

Essential Facts

- The courts are the principal avenue provided by the legal system as a means of enabling a party to vindicate his legal rights.
- Arbitration, neutral expert/neutral evaluation and mediation/conciliation are alternative means of resolving commercial disputes.
- Litigation may take place in the sheriff courts or the Court of Session.
- The rules for arbitration can be found in the comprehensive Arbitration (Scotland) Act 2010.

INDEX

bankruptcy
  diligence contrasted, 149–50
  see also **personal insolvency**
barter, 3
"basis of the contract" clauses, 55
bearer bills, 108–9
beneficium cedendarum actionum, 93
bills of exchange
  acceptor
    definition, 106
    liability, 111
  address, 107
  bearer bills, 108–9
  definition, 106–8
  discharge, 112
  dishonour, 111–12
  drawee
    definition, 106
    liability, 110–11
  drawer
    definition, 106
  enforcement, 111–12
  generally, 105
  holder
    due course, in, 110
    value, for, 109–10
  indorsee
    definition, 106
  indorsement
    generally, 106
    specified payee bills, 109
  indorser
    enforcement against, 112
    generally, 106
  liability on, 110–11
  negotiation, 104–6
  non-acceptance, 113
  order of specified person, 108
  parties, 106
  payable on demand, 108
  payee, 106
  presentment
    excused, 113
    generally, 113
    payment, for, 113–14

  signature, 107
  specified payee bills
    indorsement, 109
    negotiation, 108–9
  sum certain in money, 108
  writing, in, 107
bills of lading, 70, 105
buyer of goods
  consumer, 1–2
  definition, 3
  duties, 16
  remedies
    consumer, as, 18–20
    damages, 13–14
    generally, 12–13
    non-consumer, as, 13–16
    price reduction, 19
    rejection, 14–16, 18, 19–20
    repair or replacement, 19

calling up standard securities, 77–8
cautionary obligations
  accessory nature, 88–90
  cautioner
    liability of, 92
    rights of, 92–4
  co-cautioners
    discharge of, 95–6
    generally, 88
  constitution, 87–8
  extent of caution, 92
  form, 87–8
  generally, 87
  "giving time", 95
  improper cautionry, 90
  indemnity distinguished, 88–9
  misrepresentation, 90–2
  parties, 87
  proper cautionry, 90
  security
    giving up, 96
    sharing in, cautioner's right, 93
  termination
    cautioner, by, 96

EU representative:
Easy Access System Europe
Mustamäe tee 50, 10621 Tallinn, Estonia
Gpsr.requests@easproject.com

www.ingramcontent.com/pod-product-compliance
Lightning Source LLC
Chambersburg PA
CBHW070351200326
41518CB00012B/2209